COGAT®
TEST PREP
GRADE 7 & GRADE 8

COGAT® TEST PREP
GRADE 7 & GRADE 8
Level 13 / Level 14

Gateway Gifted Resources™
www.GatewayGifted.com

PLEASE LEAVE
US A REVIEW!

Thank you for selecting this book. We are a family-owned publishing company - a consortium of educators, test designers, book designers, parents, and kid-testers.

We would be thrilled if you left us a quick review on the website where you purchased this book!

The Gateway Gifted Resources™ Team
www.GatewayGifted.com

TABLE OF CONTENTS

ABOUT THIS BOOK: This book helps prepare kids for the COGAT® Level 13/14, a test given to seventh/ eighth graders. Not only will this help prepare kids for the COGAT®, these logic-based exercises may also be used for other gifted test preparation and as critical thinking exercises. This book has five parts.

1. Introduction (p.4-9): About this book & the COGAT®, Test Taking Tips, and Question Examples

2. Practice Test 1 (Workbook Format): These pages are designed similarly to content tested in the COGAT®'s nine test question types. Unless you already have experience with COGAT® prep materials, you should complete Practice Test 1 (Workbook Format) together with no time limit. **Before doing this section, read the Question Examples & Explanations (p.5).**

3. Practice Test 2: Practice Test 2 helps kids develop critical thinking and test-taking skills. It provides an introduction in a relaxed manner (parents provide guidance if needed) and an opportunity for kids to focus on a group of questions for a longer time period. This part is also a way for you to identify points of strength/ challenges in COGAT® question types. Practice Test 2 is divided into three sections to mirror the three COGAT® batteries: Verbal, Quantitative, and Non-Verbal.

4. **Answer Keys:** These pages contain the Practice Test answers as well as brief answer explanations.

ABOUT THE COGAT® LEVEL 13/14: The COGAT® (Cognitive Abilities Test®) test is divided into 3 batteries.

- *Verbal Battery; total time: around 45 minutes*

Question Types (15 minutes each, approximately): Verbal Analogies, Verbal Classification, Sentence Completion

- *Non-Verbal Battery; total time: around 45 minutes*

Question Types (15 minutes each, approximately): Figure Analogies, Figure Classification, Paper Folding

- *Quantitative Battery; total time: around 45 minutes*

Question Types (15 minutes each, approximately): Number Series, Number Puzzles, Number Analogies

The test has 176 questions total. The test is administered in different testing sessions. Kids are not expected to finish 176 questions in one session.

ABOUT **COGAT®** TESTING PROCEDURES: These vary by school. Tests may be given individually or in a group. These tests may be used as the single factor for admission to gifted programs, or they may be used in combination with IQ tests or as part of a student "portfolio." They are used by some schools together with tests like Iowa Assessments™. Check with your testing site to determine its specific testing procedures.

QUESTION NOTE: Because each person has different cognitive abilities, the questions in this book are at varied skill levels. The exercises may or may not require a great deal of parental guidance to complete, depending on your kid's abilities, prior test prep experience, or prior testing experience. Most sections of the Workbook begin with a relatively easy question. We suggest always completing at least the first question together, ensuring there's not any confusion about what the question asks or with the directions.

SCORING NOTE: Check with your school/program for its scoring procedure and admissions requirements. Here is a general summary of the COGAT® scoring process. First, your child's raw score is established. This is the number of questions correctly answered. Points are not deducted for questions answered incorrectly. Next, this score is compared to other test-takers of his/her same age group (and, for the COGAT®, the same grade level) using various indices to then calculate your child's stanine (a score from one to nine) and percentile rank. If your child achieved the percentile rank of 98%, then (s)he scored as well as or better than 98% of test-takers. In general, gifted programs accept scores of *at least* 98% or *higher*. Please note that a percentile rank "score" cannot be obtained from our practice material. This material has not been given to a large enough sample of test-takers to develop any kind of base score necessary for percentile rank calculations.

QUESTION EXAMPLES & EXPLANATIONS   This section introduces the nine COGAT® question types with very simple examples/explanations. Questions in Practice Test 1 & 2 will be more challenging than those below.

1. VERBAL ANALOGIES Directions: Look at the first set of words. Try to figure out how they belong together. Next, look at the second set of words. The answer is missing. Figure out which answer choice would make the second set go together in the same way that the first set goes together.

toe > foot : petal > ?   stem   bee   leg   flower   colorful

Explanation: Here are some strategies to help select the correct answer:
• Try to come up with a "rule" describing how the first set goes together. Take this rule, apply it to the first word in the second set. Determine which answer choice makes the second set follow the same "rule." If more than one choice works, you need a more specific rule. Here, a "rule" for the first set is that 'the first word (toe) is part of the second word (foot)." In the next set, using this rule, "flower" is the answer. A petal is part of a flower.
• Another strategy is to come up with a sentence describing how the first set of words go together. A sentence would be: A toe is part of a foot. Then, take this sentence and apply it to the word in the second set: A petal is part of a ?. Figure out which answer choice would best complete the sentence. (It would be "flower.")
• Ensure you do not choose a word simply because it *has to do with* the first set. For example, choice A ("stem") *has to do with* a petal, but does not follow the rule.

The simple examples will introduce you to analogical thinking. Read the "Question" then "Answer Choices". Which choice goes best? (The answer is underlined.)

Analogy Logic	Question	Answer Choices (Answer is Underlined)			
• Antonyms	On *is to* Off -as- Hot *is to* ?	Warm	Sun	<u>Cold</u>	Oven
• Synonyms	Big *is to* Large -as- Horrible *is to* ?	Tired	Stale	Sour	<u>Awful</u>
• Whole: Part	Tree *is to* Branch -as- House *is to* ?	Street	Apartment	<u>Room</u>	Home
• Degree	Good *is to* Excellent -as- Tired *is to* ?	Boring	<u>Exhausted</u>	Drowsy	Slow
• Object: Location	Sun *is to* Sky -as- Swing *is to* ?	<u>Playground</u>	Monkey Bars	Sidewalk	Grass
• Same Animal Class	Turkey *is to* Parrot -as- Ant *is to* ?	Worm	<u>Beetle</u>	Duck	Spider
• Object: Creator	Painting *is to* Artist -as- Furniture *is to* ?	<u>Carpenter</u>	Tool	Chair	Potter
• Object: Container	Ice Cube *is to* Ice Tray -as- Flower *is to* ?	Petal	<u>Vase</u>	Smell	Florist
• Tool: Worker	Paintbrush *is to* Artist -as- Microscope *is to* ?	Telescope	<u>Scientist</u>	Lab	Fireman
• Object: 3D Shape	Ball *is to* Sphere -as- Dice *is to* ?	Line	Square	Cone	<u>Cube</u>
• Object: Location Used	Jet *is to* Sky -as- Canoe *is to* ?	Boat	Paddle	<u>Water</u>	Sail
• Object: Location Used	Chalk *is to* Chalkboard -as- Paintbrush *is to* ?	Artist	<u>Easel</u>	Paint	Eraser

2. VERBAL CLASSIFICATION Directions: Look at the three words on the top row. Figure out how the words are alike. Next, look at the words in the answer choices. Which word goes best with the three words in the top row?

cake   bread   muffin

A. bakery   B. sherbet   C. cookie   D. syrup   E. sugar

Explanation: Come up with a "rule" describing how they're alike. Then, see which answer choice follows the rule. If more than one choice does, you need a more specific rule.
• At first, test-takers may say the rule for the top words is that "they are all a kind of food." However, more than one answer choice would fit this rule. A more specific rule is needed. A more specific rule would be that "the foods are baked foods." Therefore, the best answer is "cookie."
• Ensure you do not choose a word simply because it has to do with the top three. For example, choice A (bakery) has to do with the three, as all three could be found at a bakery. However, "bakery" is not a baked food. Another simple example:

fall   spring   summer

A. warm   B. season   C. month   D. winter   E. weather

This example demonstrates a common mistake. Note answer choice "B", season. Here, the question logic (or, rule) is "seasons." A test-taker, having the rule "seasons" in their mind, may mistakenly choose "season." However, the answer is "winter," because "winter," like the top three words, is an *example* of a season.

3. SENTENCE COMPLETION Directions: First, read the sentence. There is a missing word. Which answer choice goes best in the sentence?

If you aren't _____ with the vase, it will break.
A. careless   B. careful   C. clear   D. risky   E. sloppy

Explanation: Here, you must use the information in the sentence and make inferences (i.e., make a best guess based on the information) and select the best answer choice to fill in the blank. Be sure to:
• pay attention to each word in the sentence and to each answer choice
• after making a choice, re-read the complete sentence to ensure the choice makes the *most* sense compared to the other choices (the answer is B)

4. FIGURE ANALOGIES Directions: Look at the top set of pictures. They go together in some way. Look at the bottom set. The answer is missing. Figure out which answer choice would make the bottom set go together in the same way that the top set goes together.

Explanation: Come up with a "rule" describing how the top set is related. This "rule" shows how the figures in the left box "change" into the figures in the right box. On the left are 2 pentagons. On the right are 3 pentagons. The rule/change is that one more of the same kind of shape is added. On the bottom are 2 rectangles. The first choice is incorrect, it shows 3 pentagons (not the same shape). The second choice is incorrect (it only shows 2 rectangles). The third choice is incorrect - it has 2 pentagons. The last choice is correct. It has one more of the same shapes from the left box.

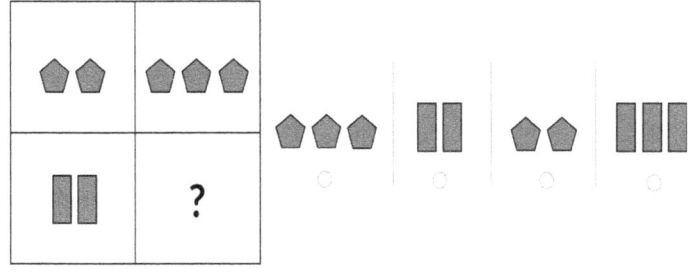

Here's another simple example:

In the top left box, we see 1 star. In the top right box, we also see a star, but it has gotten bigger. Let's come up with a rule to describe how the picture has changed from left to right. From left to right, the shape gets bigger. The last choice follows the rule. It is the same shape as the bottom box, but it is bigger.

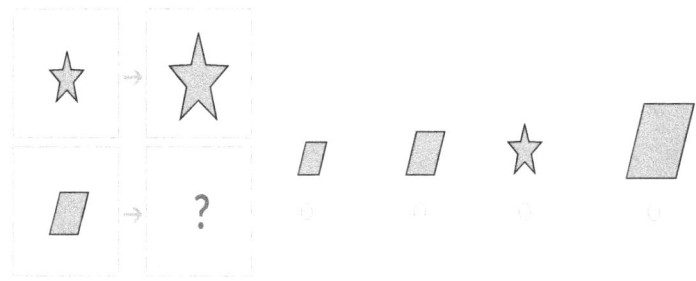

Here's another example:
In the top left box, we see a heart. In the top right box, the heart rotates 180 degrees and a vertical line is added in the center. Look at the bottom left box and the answer choices. Which answer choice follows this rule? It's C.

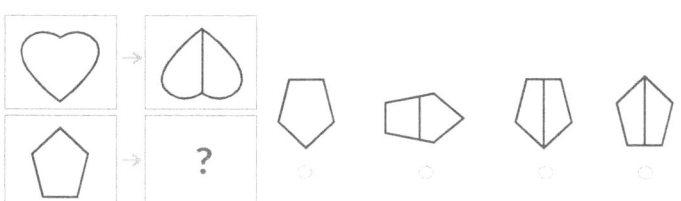

This last one is more challenging. In the top left box we see a larger square with vertical, curvy lines and a smaller square with straight, diagonal lines going from upper left to lower right. This smaller square aligns with the left corner of the larger square. In the top right box, we see the same 2 squares, but what has changed? The smaller square is now aligned with the right corner of the larger square (instead of the left corner).

Also, the diagonal lines have changed. They are going from lower left to upper right. The larger square has not changed. The rule is the smaller shape shifts from left to right and the lines inside switch directions. The larger shape does not change. The answer where we see this rule is choice B.

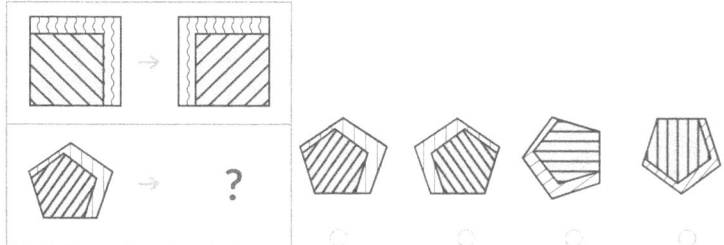

• Below are examples of basic "changes" seen in Figure Analogies.

Basic questions, like #1-#9 below, have one "change." Questions at the Grade 7/8 level will have at least two changes and/or changes that are not obvious. The questions in the book's two practice tests will be much more challenging than these. This is simply an intro.

1.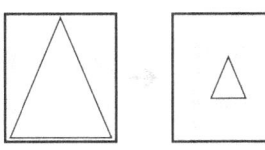

2.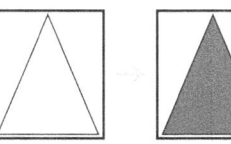

3.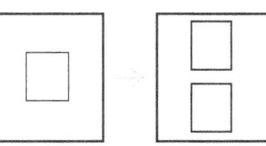

4.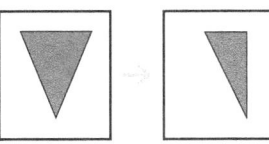

5.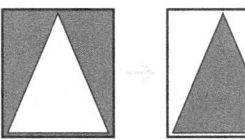

6.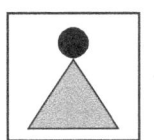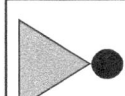

7.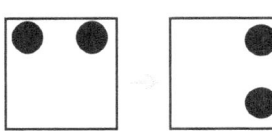

8.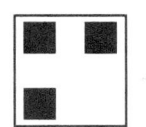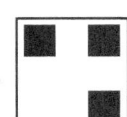

9.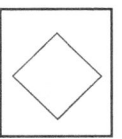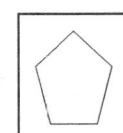

10.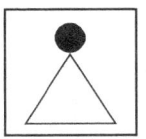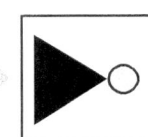

1. Size (gets smaller)
2. Color (white to gray)
3. Quantity (plus 1)
4. Whole to Half
5. Color Reversal
6. Rotation (clockwise, 90°)

7. Rotation (clockwise, 90°)
8. Rotation -or- Mirror Image / "Flip"
9. Number of Shape Sides (shape with +1 side)
10. Two Changes: Rotation (clockwise, 90°)
    and Color Reversal

5. FIGURE CLASSIFICATION

Directions: The top row shows three pictures that are alike in some way. Look at the bottom row. There are four pictures. Which picture in the bottom row goes best with the pictures in the top row?

Explanation: Figure out a "rule" describing how the top pictures are alike and belong together. Then, apply the "rule" to each answer choice to determine which one follows it. If you find that more than one choice follows the rule, then a more specific rule is needed.

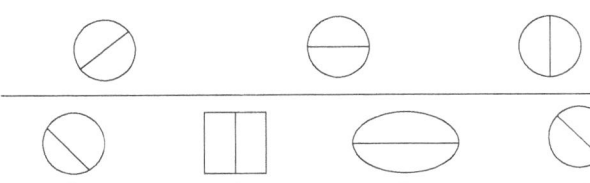

Can you come up with a rule describing how the 3 shapes are alike? They are all circles that are divided in half. In the bottom row, which choice follows this rule? Choice A is a circle, but it's not divided in half. Choice B and C are divided in half, but they are not circles. Choice D is a circle divided in half. Choice D is the answer.

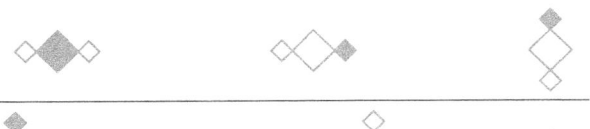

Can you come up with a rule for this one? Here, in the group of 3 diamonds, there is 1 dark diamond and 2 light diamonds. Which one of the answer choices follows this rule? Choice C.

This list outlines some basic logic in Figure Classification questions. (Practice test questions will be more challenging.)

How shapes are divided (Here, shapes are divided in quarters, with 1 part filled in.)	
How many sides the shapes have (Here, it is 4.)	
Do shapes have all rounded corners or straight corners? Or, no corners at all?	
Direction shapes are facing (Here, they face right.)	
Color / Design inside shape (Here, there are dots.)	
Shape quantity in each shape group (Here, 2 shapes in each group.)	
Shape group, with a set order to the group (Here, it's circle-diamond-square.)	
Direction of inside lines (Here, diagonal from upper left to lower right side.)	

6. PAPER FOLDING

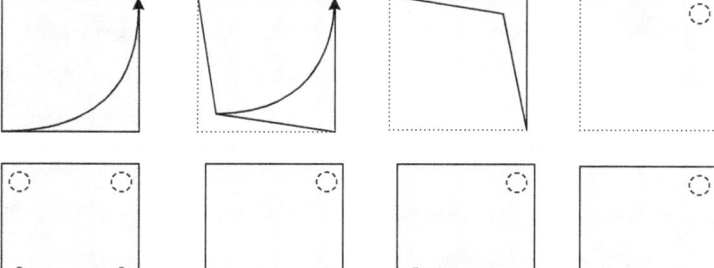

Directions: The top row of pictures shows a sheet of paper. The paper was folded, then something was cut out. Which picture in the bottom row shows how the paper would look after its unfolded?

Explanation: The first choice has too many holes. In the second choice, the holes are not in the correct position. The third choice has the correct number of holes and in the correct position. The last choice only shows the hole on top.

Tip: It is common to struggle with Paper Folding - it is not an activity most people have experience with. First, have a look at these Paper Folding examples. Then, demonstrate using real paper and scissors, if needed.

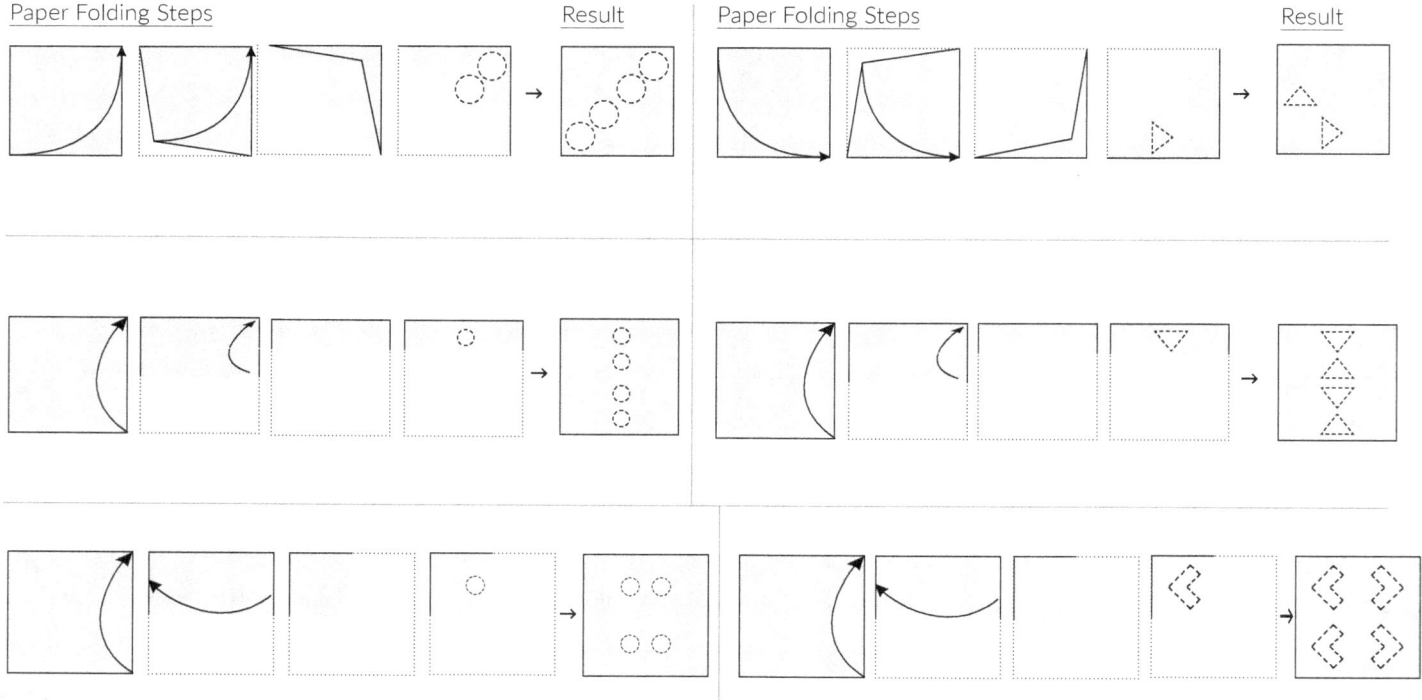

| Paper Folding Steps | Result | Paper Folding Steps | Result |

7. NUMBER SERIES (QUANTITATIVE BATTERY)

Directions: The top row of numbers have made a pattern. Which answer choice would complete the pattern?

| 6 | 9 | 12 | 15 | 18 | ? | A. 21 | B. 3 | C. 22 | D. 24 | E. 30 |

Explanation: To help see the pattern, write the difference between each number. Here, the difference between 6 and 9 is 3. The difference between 9 and 12 is 3. The difference between 12 and 15 is 3, and so on. In less challenging questions, this "difference" will be the same for each set of numbers. If the pattern is "add 3," then the answer is 21, because 18 +3 = 21. In more challenging questions, this pattern is not consistent. See below:

30	29	27	24	20	15	?	Pattern: -1, -2, -3, -4, etc.; Answer: 9
7	2	1	7	2	1	?	Pattern: 7-2-1; Answer: 7
3	4	6	7	9	10	?	Pattern: +1, +2, +1, +2, etc.; Answer: 12
5	0	6	0	7	0	?	Pattern: every other number +1; every other number=0; Ans: 8
80	160	40	80	20	40	?	Pattern: x2, divide by 4, x2, divide by 4, etc.; Ans: 10

8. NUMBER PUZZLES

Directions: Which number would replace the question mark so that both sides of the equal sign are the same?

Explanation: These questions have two formats. The first example is a standard math problem. In the second example, you need to replace the black shape with the given number. Should you have problems figuring out the answer of either format, you can simply test each answer choice until you find the correct answer.

1. $19 = ? + 5$ A. 5 B. 24 C. 20 D. 4 E. 14

2. $? = \blacksquare - 8$ A. 0 B. 1 C. 2 D. 3 E. 4
   $\blacksquare = 11$

Note: Next is a problem with 2 variables (the square and the circle). Look at the bottom row. You can solve for the circle first. 16 - 2 = 14. So, the circle = 14. Plug 14 in for the circle in the middle row. Now, you can figure out the square. The square equals 14 + 4. So, the square is 18. Next, go to the top row and plug in 18 for the square. What is 18 ÷ 2? It is 9. So, ? = 9.

3. $\blacksquare \div 2 = ?$
   $\blacksquare = 4 + \bullet$ A. 0 B. 9 C. 18 D. 6 E. 4
   $\bullet = 16 - 2$

9. NUMBER ANALOGIES

Directions: Look at the first two sets of numbers. Come up with a rule that both of these sets follow. Use this rule to figure out which answer choice goes in place of the question mark in the last set of numbers.

[2 → 6] [4 → 12] [10 → ?] A. 6 B. 3 C. 13 D. 30 E. 7

Explanation: Figure out a rule that explains how the first number "changes" into the second number. It could use addition, subtraction, multiplication, or division. Write the rule by *each* pair. Make sure this rule works with *both* pairs. The rule is "multiply by 3", so 30 is the answer.

Note: There could also be 2 operations involved in the analogy. The below analogy, for example, involves multiplication as the first step and subtraction for the second step. Here, you must multiply by 2, then subtract 1. For example, in the first analogy, 2 x 2 = 4. Then, 4 -1= 3. In the second analogy, 4 x 2 = 8. Then, 8 - 1 = 7. So, 5 x 2 = 10. Then, 10 - 1 = 9. (Choice E.)

[2 → 3] [4 → 7] [5 → ?] A. 6 B. 8 C. 11 D. 10 E. 9

HINTS PAGE

- COGAT® questions can be quite challenging.

- This page lists the logic (not the answers, just the logic) involved in solving some of the questions in: Verbal Classification & Analogies, Figure Classification & Analogies, and Number Analogies & Number Series.

- If this is your student's first time with COGAT® prep, you may wish to **cut out this page** and allow them to use it as they tackle these tricky questions for the first time.

Verbal Classification
1. type of animal
2. type of job
3. similar number
4. parts of a book
5. similar adjectives

Verbal Analogies
1. type of order
2. object > purpose
3. opposites
4. use in the past vs. today
5. large form vs. very small form

Figure Classification
1. shape type & position
2. direction
3. design inside shape
4. number of sides
5. shape type & color

Figure Analogies
1. rotation
2. number of shape sides
3. color switch
4. flip/mirror image & movement
5. flip/mirror image

Number Analogies
1. multiply
2. divide
3. squared
4. divide
5. decimal & equivalent fraction

Number Series
1. multiply
2. subtract
3. look at every other number -and- add
4. subtract (different numbers) (it is not consistent)
5. add (different numbers) (it is not consistent)

Check out our other books for
COGAT® K to Grade 6

www.GatewayGifted.com

 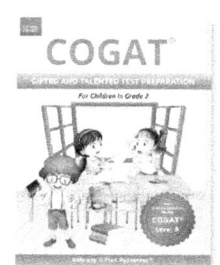 

TEST-TAKING TIPS

COGAT® Checklist (tips for answering questions)

✓ **#1: Do not rush.** Look carefully at the question and each answer choice.

✓ **#2: Use process of elimination.** You receive points for the number of correct answers. You will not lose points for incorrect answers. Instead of leaving a question unanswered, at least guess. First, eliminate any answers that are obviously not correct. Then, guess from those remaining.

✓ **#3: Double check.** Before marking your answer, double check it by going through the question and answer to make sure it makes sense. "Talking" silently to yourself as you go through it is a good idea.

✓ **#4: Be sure to choose only ONE answer.** When you fill in your bubble sheet, fill in only ONE bubble per question - instead of making a careless mistake and filling in two.

• Be sure to read the first section at the beginning of each group of questions in Practice Test 1. These have even more tips specific for each question type. They also have reminders to follow the "COGAT® Checklist" above.

Common Sense Tips

• **Get enough sleep.** This one is so obvious, yet so important. Studies have shown a link between not getting enough sleep and lower test scores.

• **Eat a breakfast for sustained energy and concentration.** (complex carbohydrates and protein; avoid foods/drinks high in sugar)

• **Use the restroom prior to the test.** The administrator may not allow a break during the test.

• **Don't get overly stressed.** Try not to worry about preparing for the test or the test itself. Instead, focus on doing your best. The test will have challenging questions, and sometimes, you will simply not know the answer. When this happens, instead of worrying, remain focused on answering the question the best you can and using the process of elimination (outlined above).

VERBAL CLASSIFICATION

Directions: Look at the three words on the top row. Figure out how the words are alike. Next, look at the words in the row of answer choices. Which word goes best with the three words in the top row?

Note: Try to come up with a "rule" to describe how the top three words are alike and go together. Then, take this "rule," and figure out which of the answer choices would best follow that same rule. If none of the choices work, you need to try a different rule. If more than one choice would work, then come up with a rule that is more specific. (See example below.)

- If you haven't read the Verbal Classification examples on page 5, do so now.
- Also, make sure to go through the checklist at the top of page 11.
- If you need some help with the first few, there is a "hints" section for Verbal Classification on page 10.

Example (#1): Let's start with an easy one. How do the words "falcon", "osprey", and "condor" go together? What is a rule that describes how they go together?

These are all kinds of birds.

However, with this rule, we can see that more than one answer choice could be correct. We need a more specific rule.

These are all kinds of birds, and they are birds of prey.

Using this more specific rule, we can see that E (hawk) is the answer. A hawk is a bird of prey.

1   **falcon**   **osprey**   **condor**

   Ⓐ ostrich   Ⓑ penguin   Ⓒ gazelle   Ⓓ sparrow   Ⓔ hawk

2   **geologist**   **biologist**   **physicist**

   Ⓐ historian   Ⓑ architect   Ⓒ chemist   Ⓓ novelist   Ⓔ entrepreneur

3   **tripod**   **trilogy**   **trident**

    A   trivial   B   triumph   C   third   D   tried   E   throng

4   **bibliography**   **preface**   **appendix**

    A   index   B   paper   C   author   D   binding   E   price

5   **robust**   **vigorous**   **potent**

    A   durable   B   fleeting   C   volatile   D   contrary   E   void

6   **replicate**   **imitate**   **simulate**

    A   originate   B   innovate   C   destroy   D   mimic   E   develop

7   **scooter**   **kayak**   **unicycle**

    A   bus   B   biplane   C   battleship   D   bullet train   E   barge

8   **jet ski**   **hot air balloon**   **yacht**

    A   surfboard   B   subway   C   tanker truck   D   submarine   E   excavator

9   **desist**   **suspend**   **abolish**

    A   conclude   B   assist   C   generate   D   ignite   E   prevail

10   **sustain**   **maintain**   **prolong**

    A   obstruct   B   abstain   C   commence   D   persist   E   prescribe

11   **expedite**   **hasten**   **precipitate**

    A   decelerate   B   accelerate   C   hinder   D   stagnate   E   aggravate

12   **meteorologist**   **climatologist**   **seismologist**

(A) nutritionist   (B) criminologist   (C) economist   (D) linguist   (E) volcanologist

13   **elevated**   **diminutive**   **lofty**

(A) minuscule   (B) solid   (C) sturdy   (D) dense   (E) spacious

14   **despondent**   **jubilant**   **apprehensive**

(A) cognizant   (B) serene   (C) tactful   (D) fractured   (E) omniscient

15   **paleontologist**   **historian**   **anthropologist**

(A) biologist   (B) chemist   (C) archaeologist   (D) linguist   (E) physicist

16   **convergence**   **unification**   **confederation**

(A) dissolution   (B) solitary   (C) synthesis   (D) fragment   (E) disperse

17   **summit**   **pinnacle**   **apex**

(A) core   (B) median   (C) depth   (D) vertex   (E) foundation

18   **republic**   **theocracy**   **oligarchy**

(A) monarchy   (B) equality   (C) capitalism   (D) administration   (E) judicial

19   **interchangeable**   **equivalent**   **congruent**

(A) autonomous   (B) synonymous   (C) distinct   (D) diverse   (E) polar

20   **plentiful**   **copious**   **myriad**

(A) sporadic   (B) finite   (C) scant   (D) singular   (E) manifold

VERBAL ANALOGIES

Directions: Look at the first set of words. They go together in some way. Next, look at the second set. Then, look at the answer choices. Which answer choice goes with the word in the second set in the same way that the first set of words goes together?

Notes: Here are two strategies for tackling verbal analogies:
• Strategy 1: Come up with a "rule" to describe how the first set is related. Then, take this "rule," use it together with the second set and figure out which of the answer choices would follow that same rule. For answer choices that do not follow it, eliminate them. If more than one choice would follow it, then come up with a rule that is more specific.

• Strategy 2: Think of a sentence that describes how the first set is related. Then, complete the same process you completed with the "rule". Apply the sentence to the answer choices. Eliminate those that do not work with the sentence. If more than one choice would work, then come up with a sentence that is more specific.

• With both strategies, you may need a different rule/sentence if the first one doesn't work. (See below.)
• If you haven't read through the Verbal Analogies examples on page 5, do so now.
• If you need some help with the first few, there is a "hints" section for Verbal Analogies on page 10.

Example (#1): How do "alphabetical" and "letter" go together? What "rule" or sentence could describe how they go together? *Rule: Alphabetical (the first word) means organized by letter (the second word). Sentence: The first word is organized according to the second word.*

Now, let's see which of the answer choices work with this rule and sentence. *Chronological (the first word) means organized by time (the second word). Things in chronological order are organized according to time.*

1   **alphabetical > letter : chronological > ?**

   A pattern   B list   C time   D calendar   E chronicle

2   **helmet > protect : sunscreen > ?**

   A moisturize   B lighten   C block   D spray   E expose

3   **expand > contract : ascend > ?**

   A hover   B trek   C elevate   D descend   E continue

4   **lantern > flashlight : telegraph > ?**

   A telephone   B communication   C teleport   D satellite   E signal

5 boulder > pebble : blaze > ?

(A) smolder   (B) vapor   (C) parched   (D) extinguish   (E) flame

6 transparent > opaque : diligent > ?

(A) hardworking   (B) careful   (C) precise   (D) industrious   (E) careless

7 brilliant > smart : deafening > ?

(A) loud   (B) quiet   (C) audible   (D) noise   (E) deaf

8 dense > mass : bright > ?

(A) dark   (B) opaque   (C) light   (D) dazzling   (E) intensity

9 documents > archive : relics > ?

(A) mine   (B) quarry   (C) excavation   (D) museum   (E) archeologist

10 breeze > gale : drizzle > ?

(A) seismic   (B) condensation   (C) drop   (D) deluge   (E) mist

11 mountain > summit : pyramid > ?

(A) base   (B) apex   (C) lateral   (D) edge   (E) triangle

12 carelessness > safety : corruption > ?

(A) rules   (B) integrity   (C) poverty   (D) authority   (E) crime

13 **curiosity > discovery : innovation > ?**

A tradition   B teamwork   C advancement   D normality   E uniformity

14 **ameliorate > improve : condense > ?**

A dissolve   B expand   C align   D magnify   E compress

15 **frugal > economical : transparent > ?**

A clear   B transformed   C obscure   D opaque   E careful

16 **fabricate > demolish : obscure > ?**

A overshadow   B reveal   C misrepresent   D ensconce   E devastate

17 **negligence > accident : disease > ?**

A health   B cure   C epidemic   D hospital   E crash

18 **preparation > readiness : training > ?**

A practice   B regulations   C prevention   D proficiency   E motivation

19 **hostile > belligerent : calm > ?**

A lethargic   B passive   C placid   D irate   E perplexed

20 **elusive > capture : enigma > ?**

A coded   B simplify   C conceal   D ponder   E solve

SENTENCE COMPLETION

Directions: First, read the sentence. There is a missing word. Next, look at the row of answer choices below the sentence. Which word would go best in the sentence?

(Note that in some sentences there is only one word missing, and you only need to choose one word. However, in others there are two words missing, and you must choose two words.)

Notes:
- Make sure to read the <u>entire</u> sentence very carefully. To ensure you have not accidentally skipped words or misread them, we suggest "mouthing" the words to yourself. You may even want to read the sentence twice.

- Eliminate answer choices that are clearly incorrect.

- Before making your final choice, read the entire sentence again using the word(s) of your answer choice. Ask yourself if these word(s) make sense in the sentence. Ask yourself if they are the best choice.

- If you have a sentence that requires two words, make sure <u>both</u> words make sense in the sentence and that they are the best choice.

1   **The students were _____ when they received the award for their hard work on the science project.**

   Ⓐ curious   Ⓑ neutral   Ⓒ confused   Ⓓ elated   Ⓔ studious

2   **Orchards and cornfields were _____ affected by the severe drought that struck the region last summer.**

   Ⓐ slightly   Ⓑ barely   Ⓒ significantly   Ⓓ somewhat   Ⓔ minimally

3   Due to the region's _____ conditions, only a few hardy species of plants and animals could survive.

   A lush   B remote   C temperate   D moderate   E barren

4   The _____ glassware should be handled with care to avoid any damage.

   A reinforced   B waterproof   C resistant   D delicate   E robust

5   The museum's vast array of _____ objects is a major draw for those interested in ancient history.

   A mundane   B rare   C modern   D contemporary   E misplaced

6   When choosing a vacation destination, he has a(n) _____ toward the mountains, citing the fresh air and serene environment.

   A bias   B conservation   C hesitation   D indifference   E reluctance

7 The groundbreaking discovery is expected to _____ the progress of renewable energy technologies.

(A) stifle   (B) regress   (C) convert   (D) bolster   (E) recycle

8 Because the soil was extremely _____, the crops failed to grow properly in the area.

(A) hydrated   (B) productive   (C) fertile   (D) organic   (E) depleted

9 The teacher assigned two _____ projects to the students, encouraging them to explore two creative approaches.

(A) identical   (B) conventional   (C) distinctive   (D) redundant   (E) predictable

10 Despite her thorough preparation, the speaker experienced a moment of _____ before going on stage.

(A) reassurance   (B) trepidation   (C) enthusiasm   (D) poise   (E) certainty

11   The athletes became _____ when they learned that their favorite coach
         would be transferring to a different school.

A dismayed   B apathetic   C elated   D hopeful   E studious

12   To _____ a novel, we must first understand the _____ of its central themes.

A publish,   B summarize,   C analyze,   D illustrate,   E critique,
   author   paragraph   irrelevance   level   significance

13   To ensure a heated argument does not _____, it's important to tackle the
         problems _____ .

A deteriorate,   B expand,   C grow,   D escalate,   E worsen,
   gradually   recklessly   passively   immediately   intermittently

14   "When you explore this area of the forest, avoid the spots with _____ terrain,"
         the park ranger _____ the hikers.

A formidable,   B uniform,   C captivating,   D ordinary,   E alluring,
   instructed   suggested   recommended   guided   recommended

15   When the young scientists presented their findings, the _____ data captured
         the audience's attention, which _____ their interest in the research.

A complex,   B groundbreaking,   C trivial,   D vague,   E deceptive,
   diminished   intensified   enhanced   inspired   supported

16 To _____ the key points of the presentation, she chose a _____ color for the final slides to stand out the most.

(A) emphasize, vibrant   (B) accentuate, pale   (C) assume, subtle   (D) highlight, muted   (E) conceal, vivid

17 The movie's storyline was enhanced by the addition of _____ challenges and complex characters with _____ personalities.

(A) routine, unremarkable   (B) familiar, elementary   (C) rare, predictable   (D) ordinary, straightforward   (E) intriguing, multifaceted

18 To _____ his personal fitness goals, it is _____ that he maintains a balanced diet and regular exercise.

(A) pursue, irrelevant   (B) achieve, trivial   (C) reach, optional   (D) realize, critical   (E) complete, redundant

19 The team members _____ in the locker room before the game, viewing the meeting as a crucial _____ for strategizing.

(A) nap, moment   (B) disperse, issue   (C) assemble, opportunity   (D) sprint, attempt   (E) break, interview

20 Although renewable energy sources are _____ in modern cities around the world, they did not _____ in earlier power systems.

(A) hidden, integrate   (B) scarce, dominate   (C) outdated, emerge   (D) prevalent, exist   (E) primitive, appear

FIGURE CLASSIFICATION

Directions: Look at the three pictures on the top row. Figure out how the pictures are alike. Next, look at the pictures in the row of answer choices. Which picture goes best with the three pictures in the top row?

Note: As you did with Verbal Classification questions, together, try to come up with a "rule" to describe how the top pictures are alike and go together. Then, take this "rule," and figure out which of the answer choices would best follow that same rule. If more than one choice follows the rule, then come up with a rule that is more specific.

• Common "rules" include (but are not limited to):
- number of sides   - color/design
- quantity   - size of figure/figure's parts
- figure order   - rounded vs. angled corners
- location of shape/shapes
- rotation or direction:
          ~ clockwise vs. counterclockwise
          ~ what degree (45°, 90°, 180°)
          ~ "flip"/mirror image

• If you haven't read the Figure Classification examples on page 7, do so now.
• If you need some help with the first few, there is a "hints" page on page 10.

Example (#1): How do these 3 shapes go together? What is a rule that describes how they go together? They are all squares, divided into four sections. There is one star in one section and one triangle in another section. However, looking at the answer choices, we see that more than one choice would be correct. So, we need a more specific rule.

Look at how the star and triangle are positioned. They are on opposite sides of each other.

Using this logic, we see that only choice D would be correct.

1

 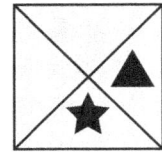 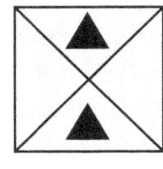 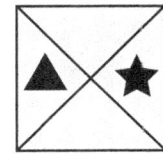 

     A   B   C   D   E

2

A B C D E

3

A B C D E

4

A B C D E

5

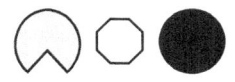  

  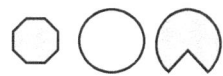  

A   B   C   D   E

6

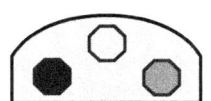 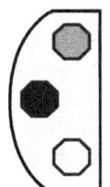 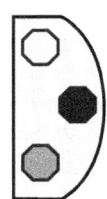

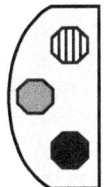 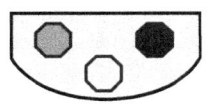 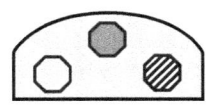  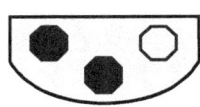

A   B   C   D   E

7

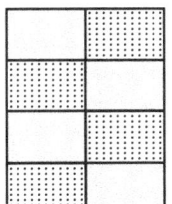 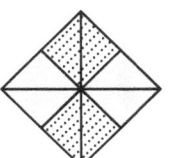 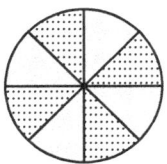

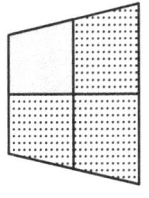 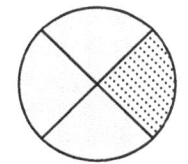 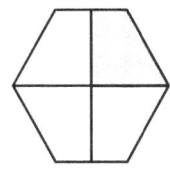 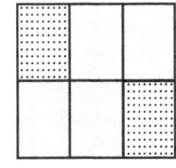 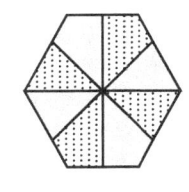

A   B   C   D   E

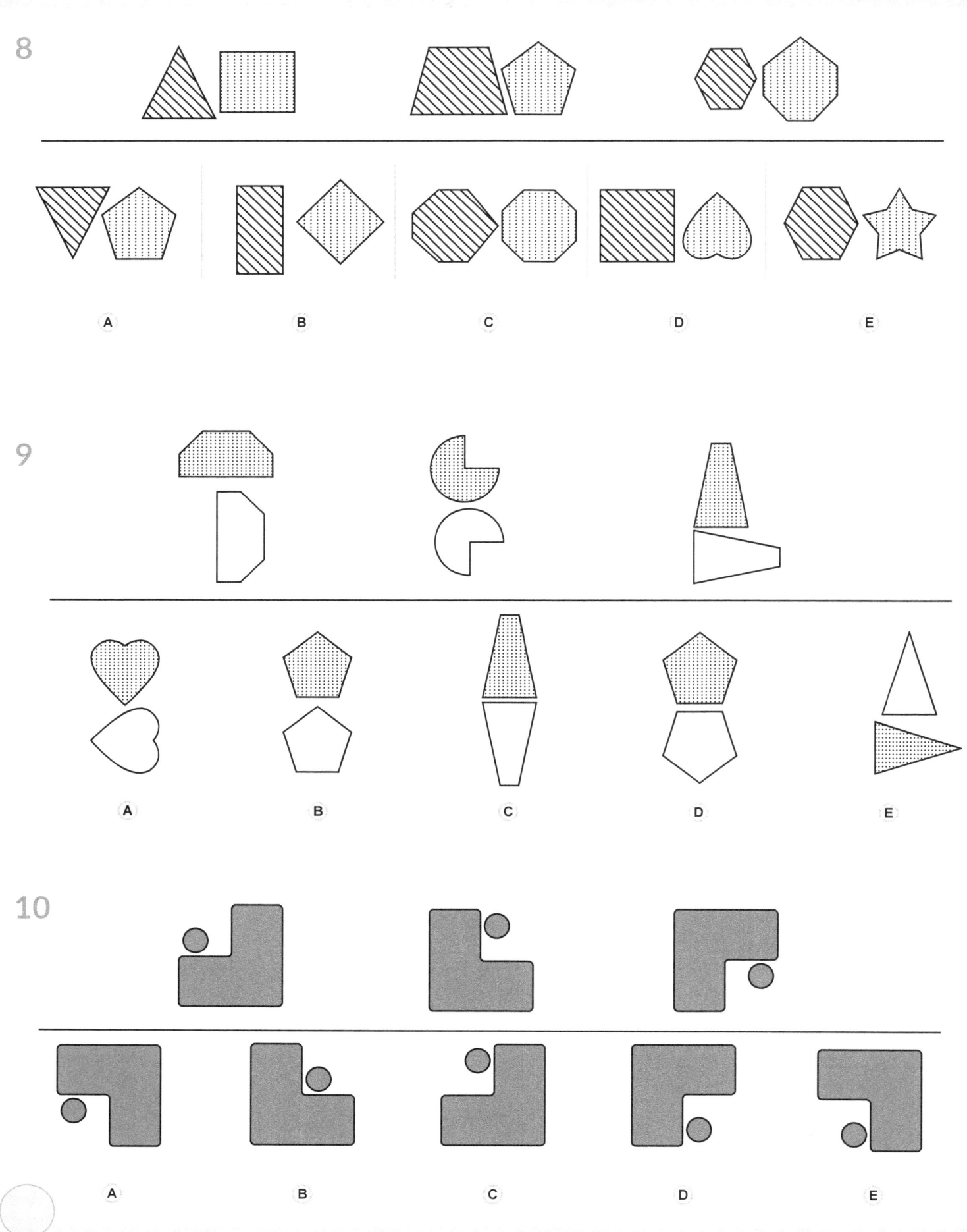

11

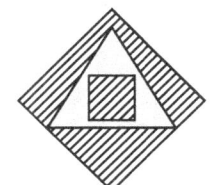  

  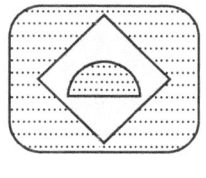 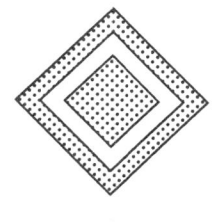

| A | B | C | D | E |

12

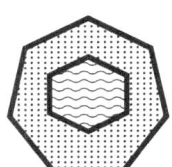 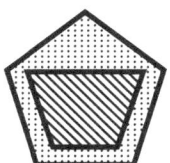 

 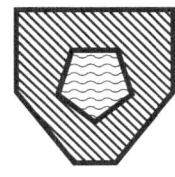   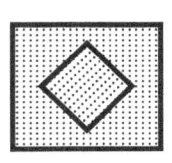

| A | B | C | D | E |

13

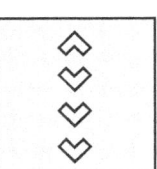 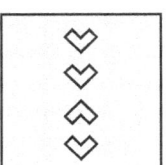 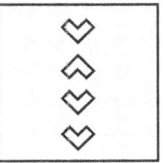

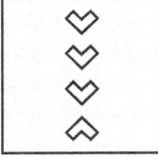

| A | B | C | D | E |

14

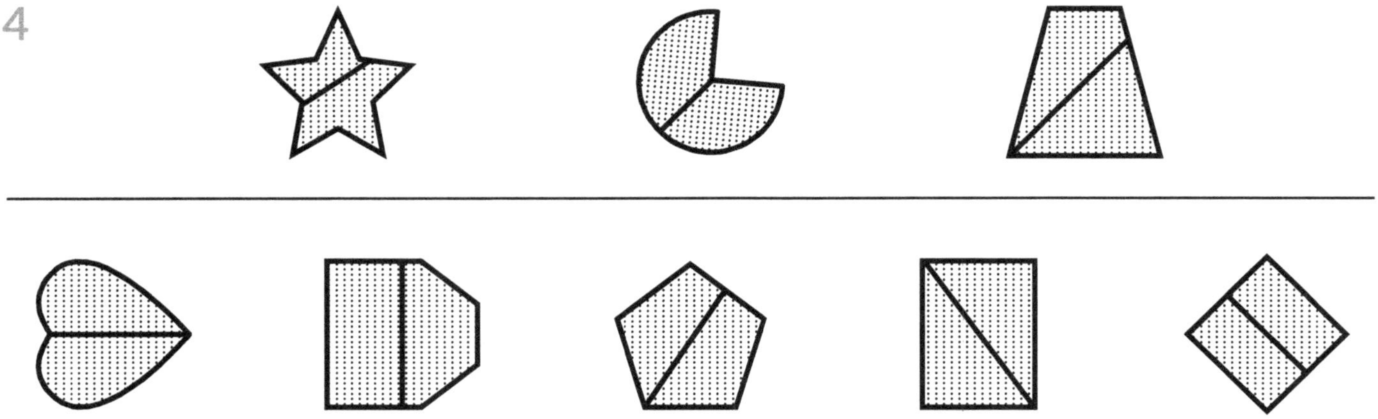

A B C D E

15

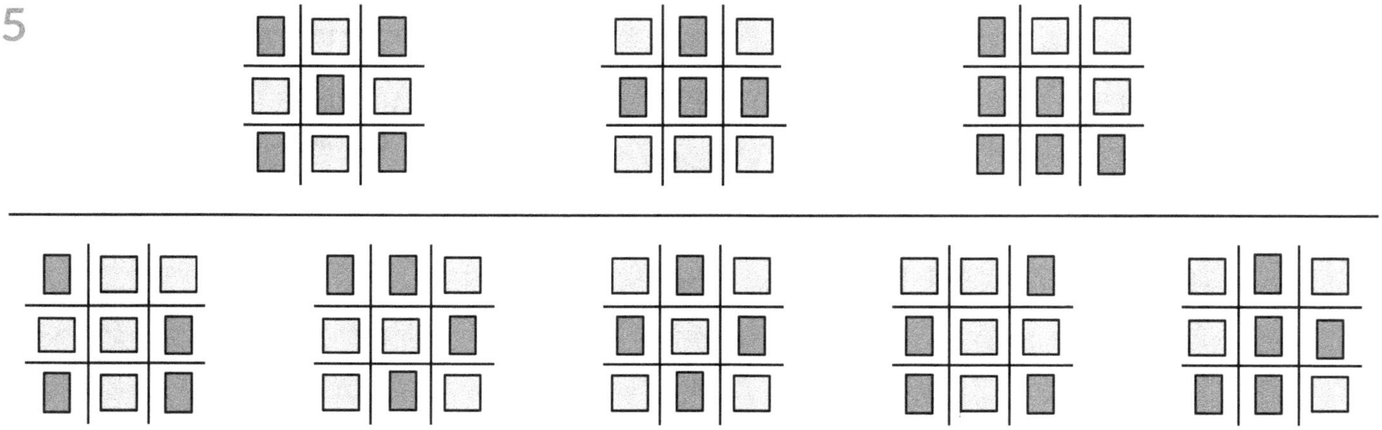

A B C D E

16

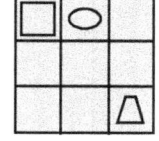 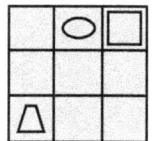 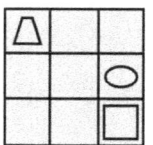

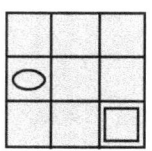 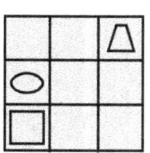 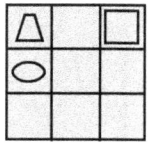 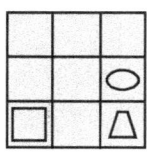 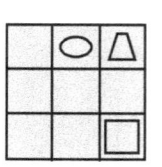

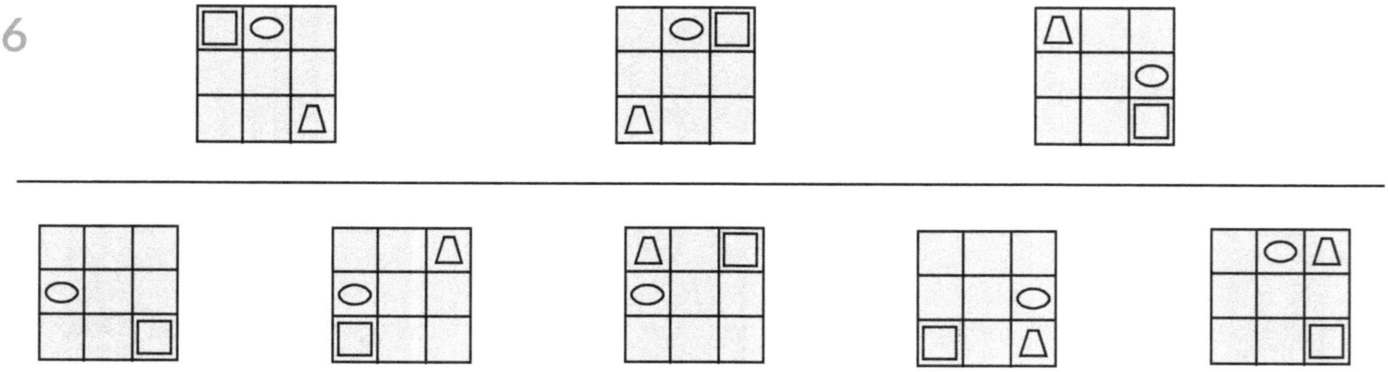

A B C D E

17

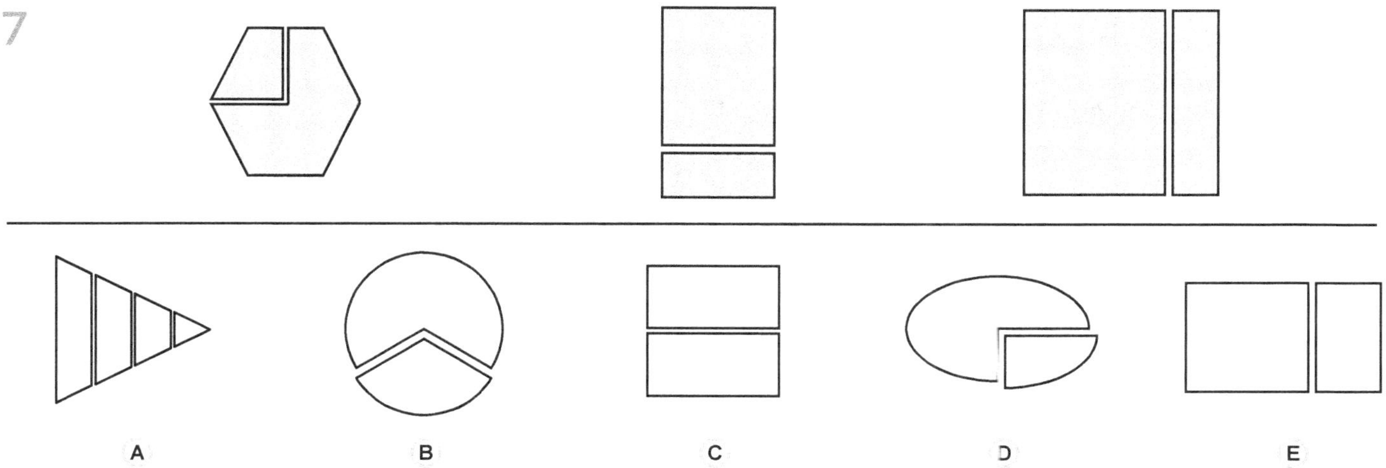

A   B   C   D   E

18

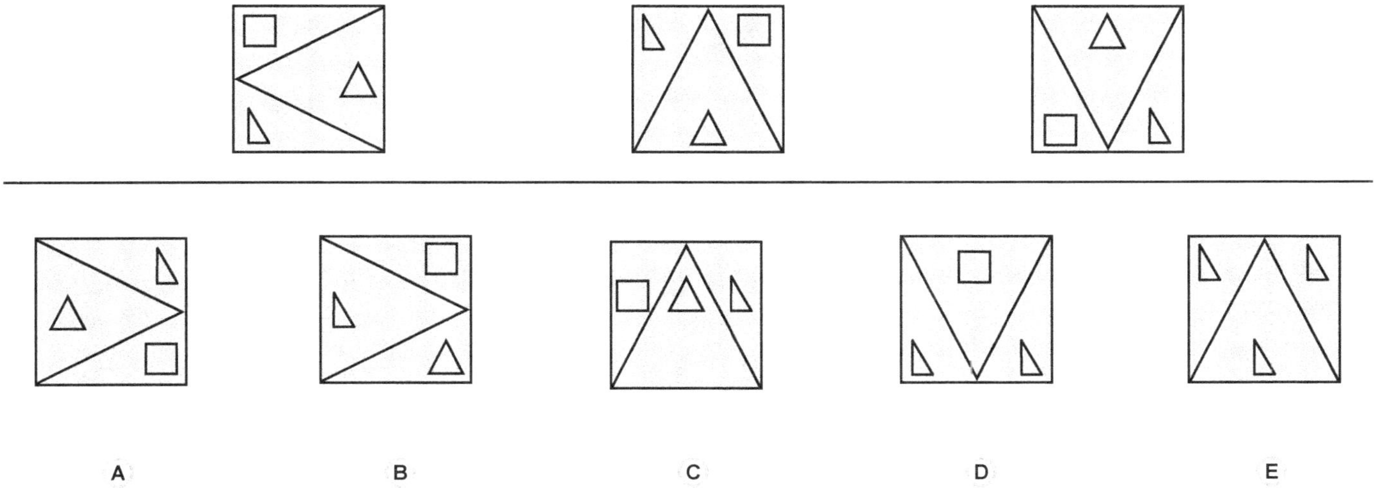

A   B   C   D   E

19

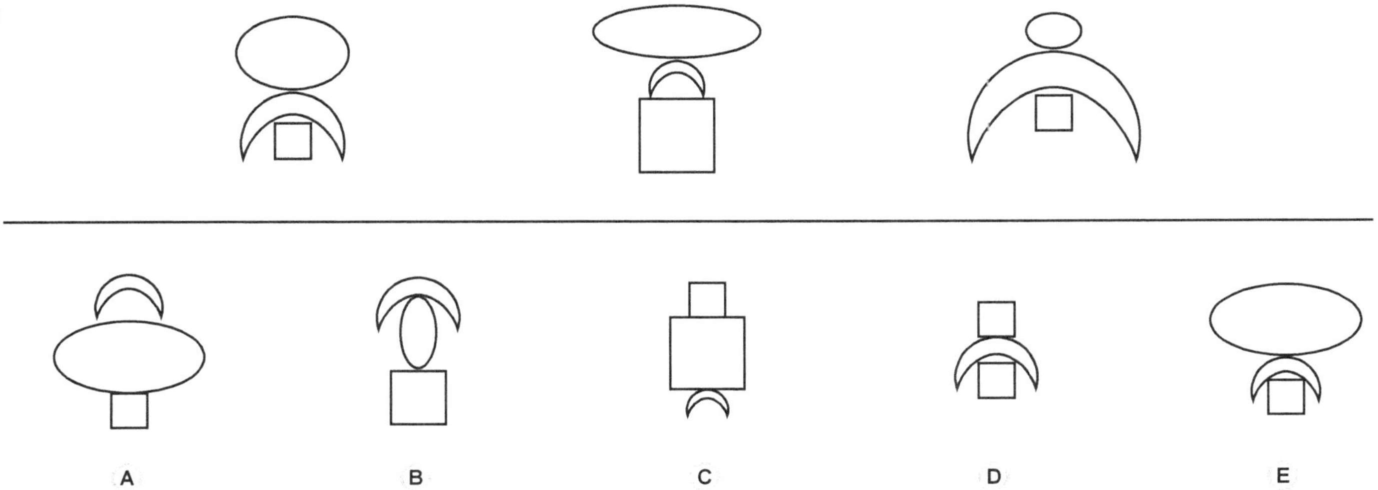

A   B   C   D   E

FIGURE ANALOGIES

Directions: Look at the top set of pictures. These belong together in some way. Next, look at the bottom picture. Then, decide which answer choice would make the bottom set of pictures go together in the same way as the top set. (The small arrow shows that the set goes together.)

Note: Use the same methodology here as Verbal Analogies. Together, come up with a "rule" to describe how the first set is related. (Tip: Try to see what "changes" from the first picture to the second picture.) Then, in the second set, look at the first picture. Take this "rule," use it together with the first picture in the second set, and figure out which of the answer choices follows it. If more than one choice follows this rule, then come up with a rule that is more specific.

• You will see similar "rules" with Figure Analogies as with Figure Classification (see p.23). As with Figure Classification, these rules will often involve more than one element. If you haven't yet read this section on p.23, do so now.

• If you haven't read the Figure Analogies examples on page 6 & page 7, do so now.

• If you need some help with the first few Figure Analogies, there is a "hints" page on page 10.

• The Answer Key explanations include additional brief explanations of "rules"/"changes".

Example (#1): In the top left box, we see a diamond that has been divided into 4 equal sections. Three of those sections are light gray and 1 is dotted. In the top right box, we see the same figure, but what has changed?

The dotted section has moved. We need to figure out how it moves. It moves clockwise by 1 section.

The rule is the dotted section moves clockwise by 1 section. The answer where we see this rule is C.

Be sure to pay close attention to the direction of rotation & the degree of rotation. Other choices also show a rotation, but they are not correct.

1

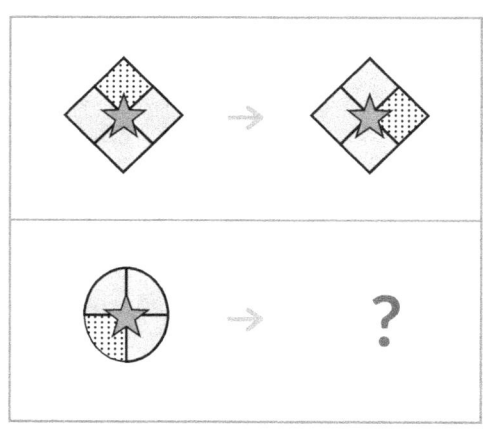

A

B

C

D

E

2

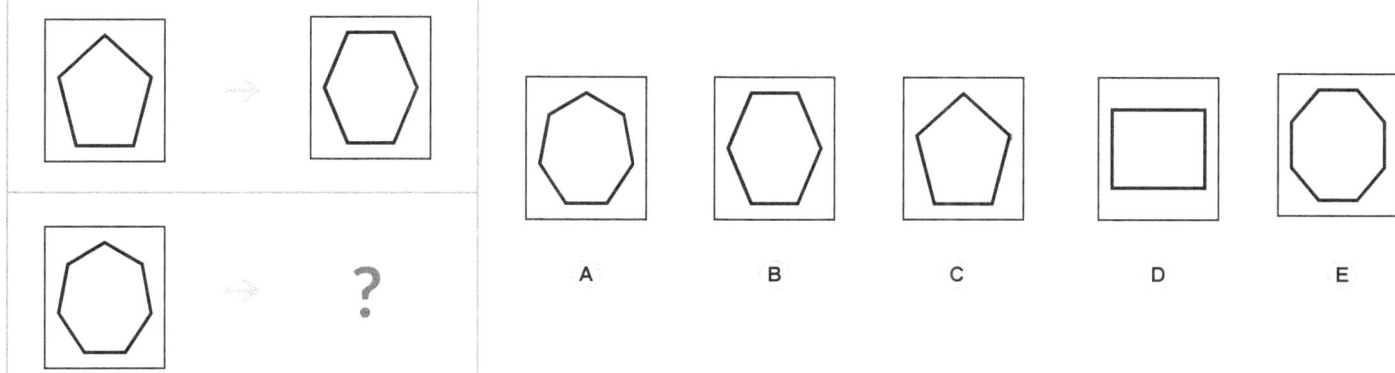

A   B   C   D   E

3

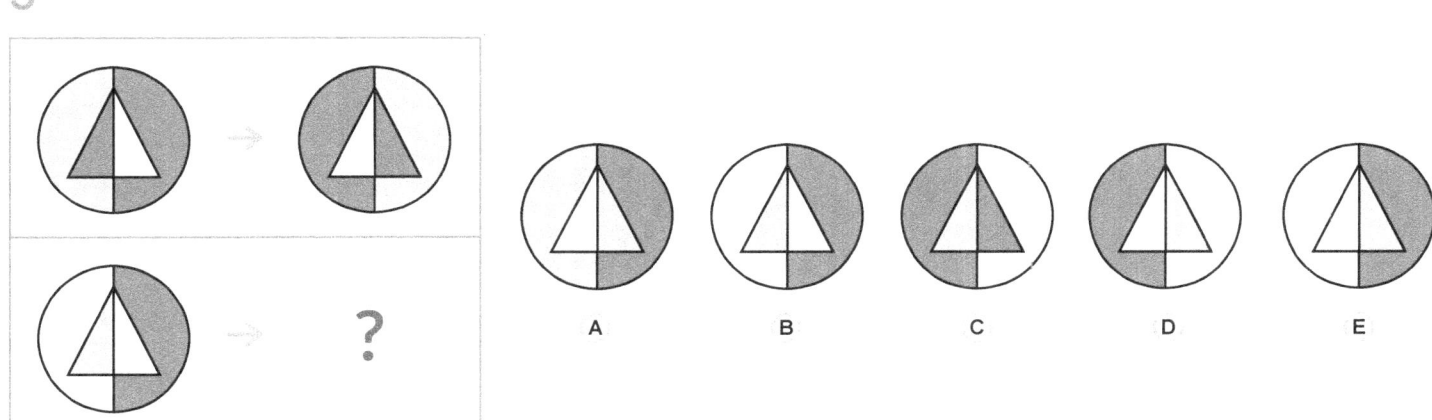

A   B   C   D   E

4

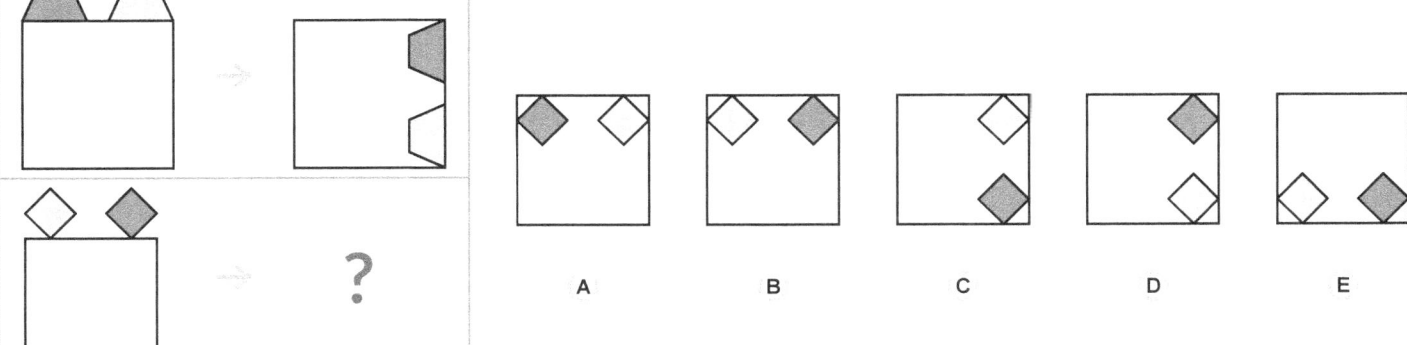

A   B   C   D   E

5

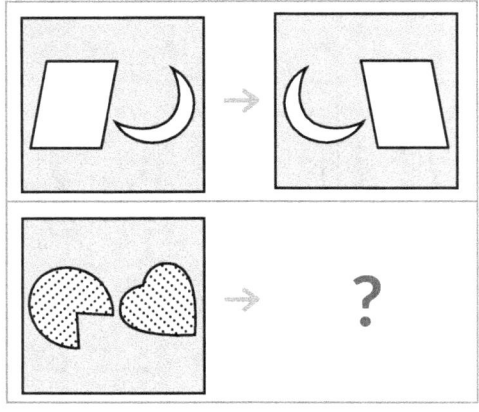

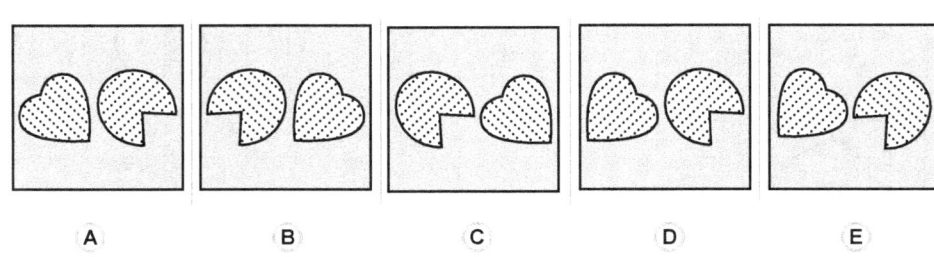

A B C D E

6

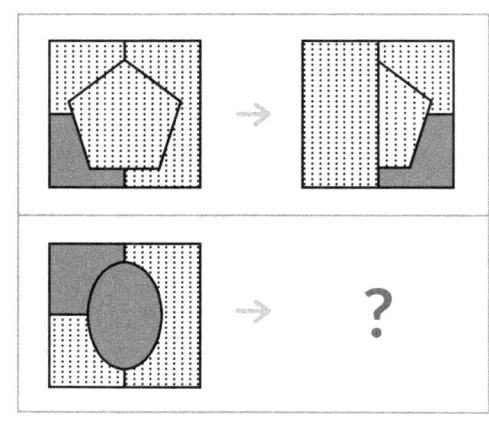

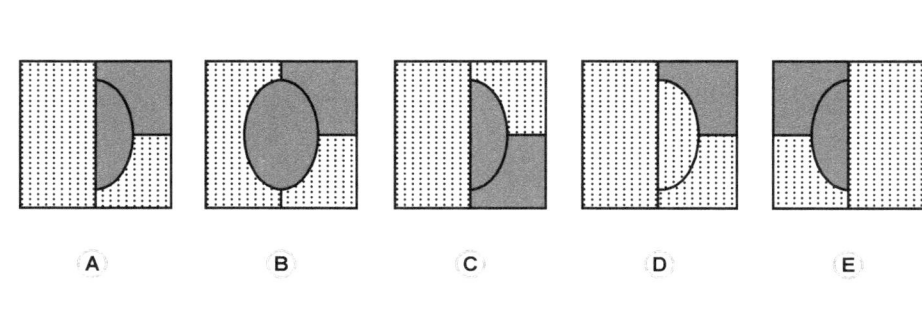

A B C D E

7

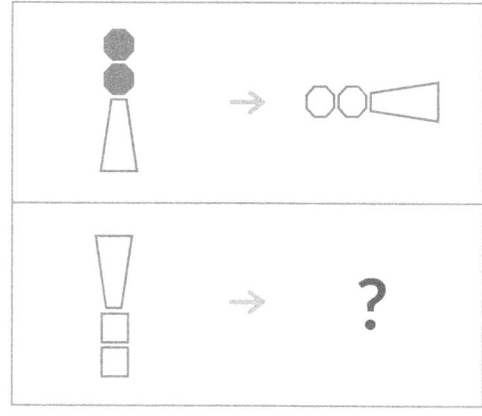

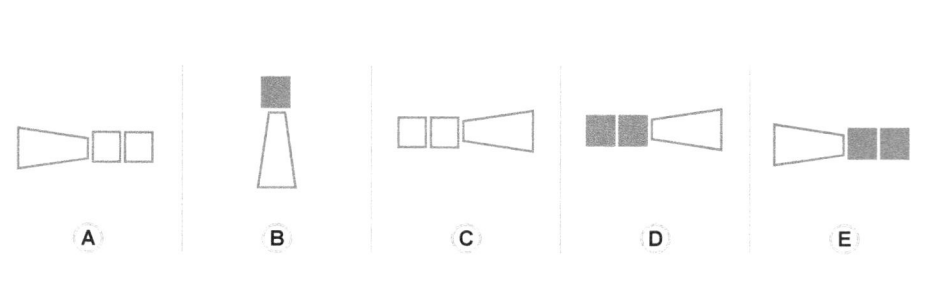

A B C D E

6

8

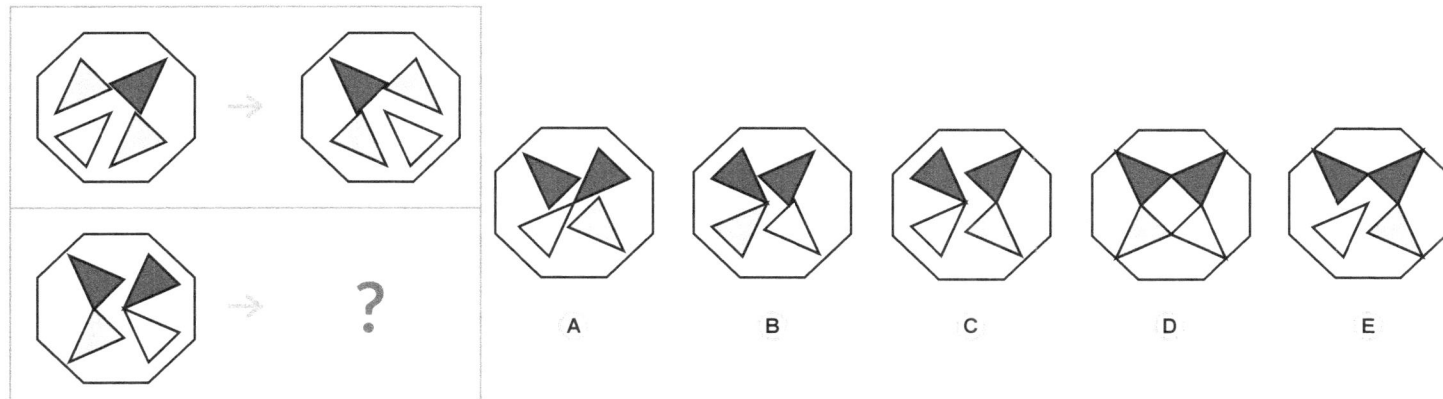

9

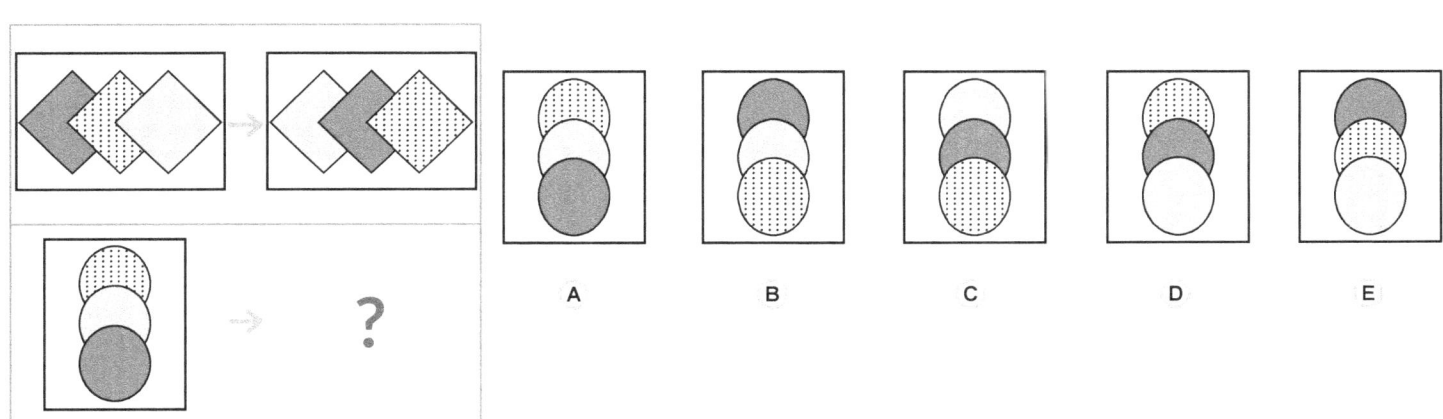

10

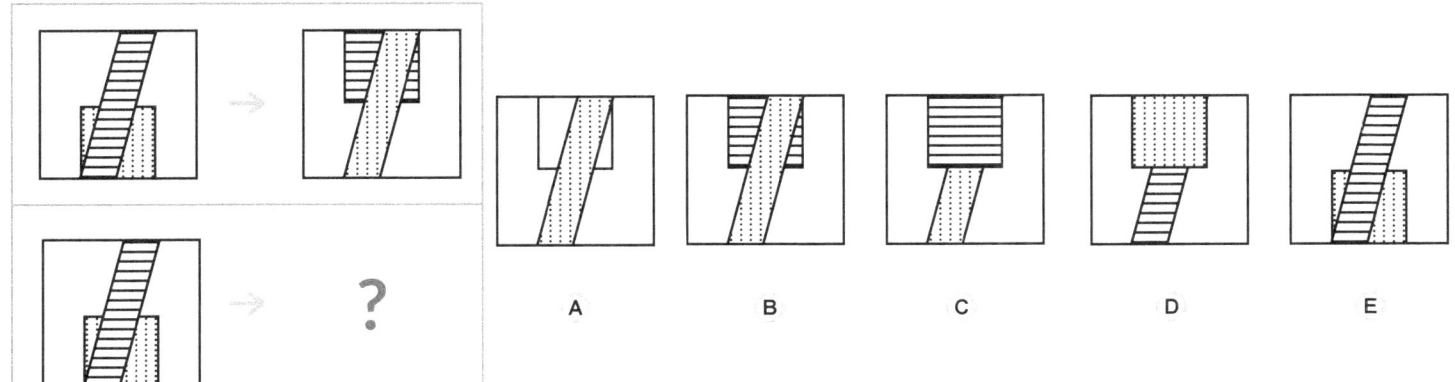

11

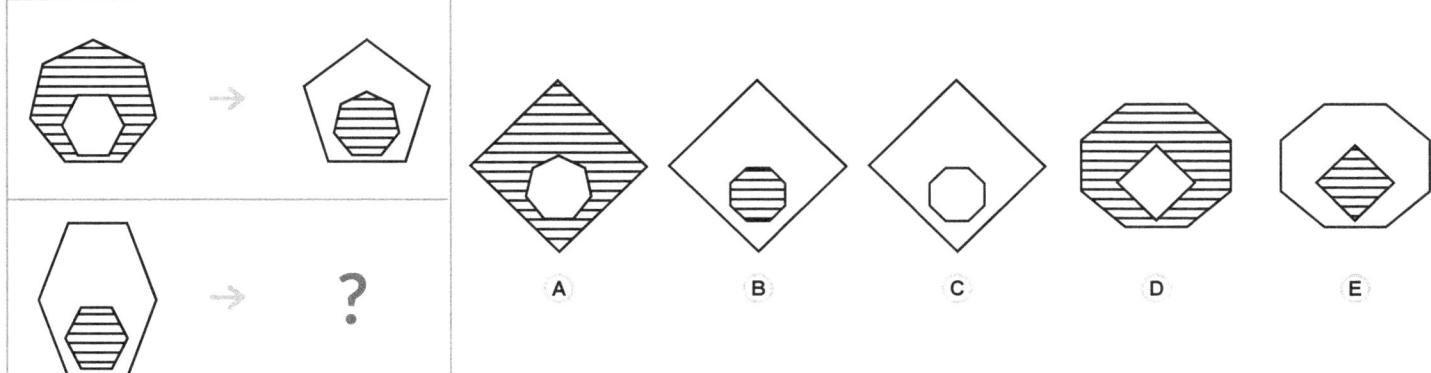

12

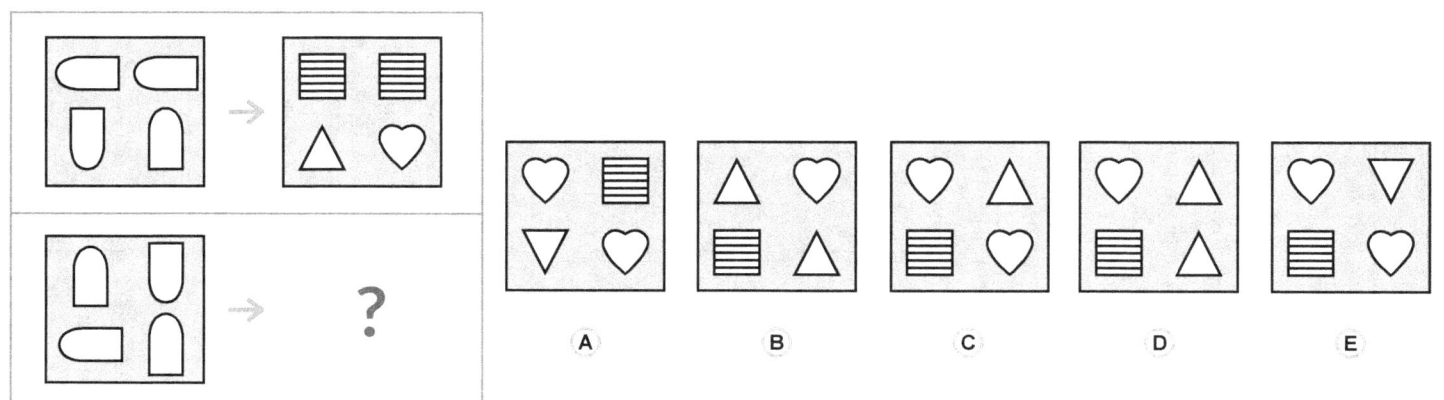

13

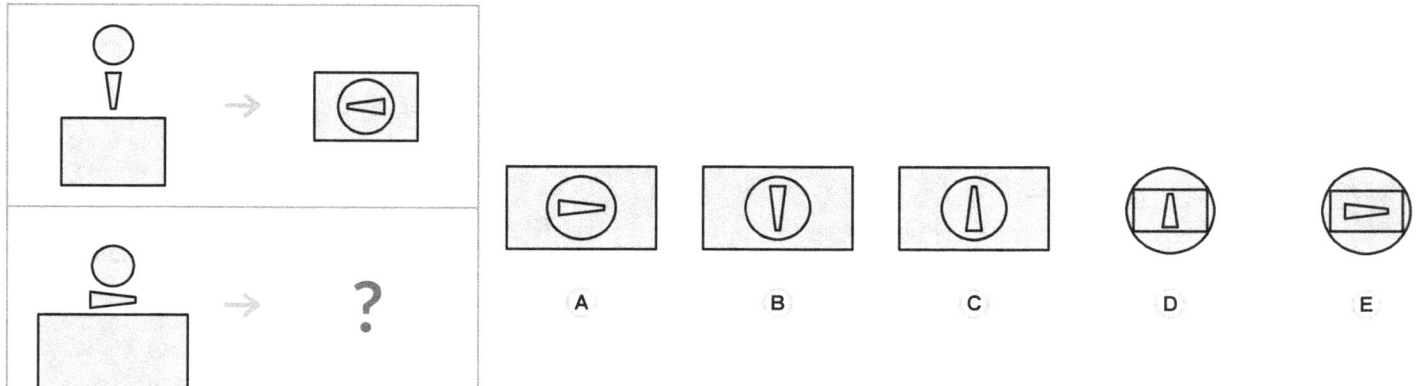

14

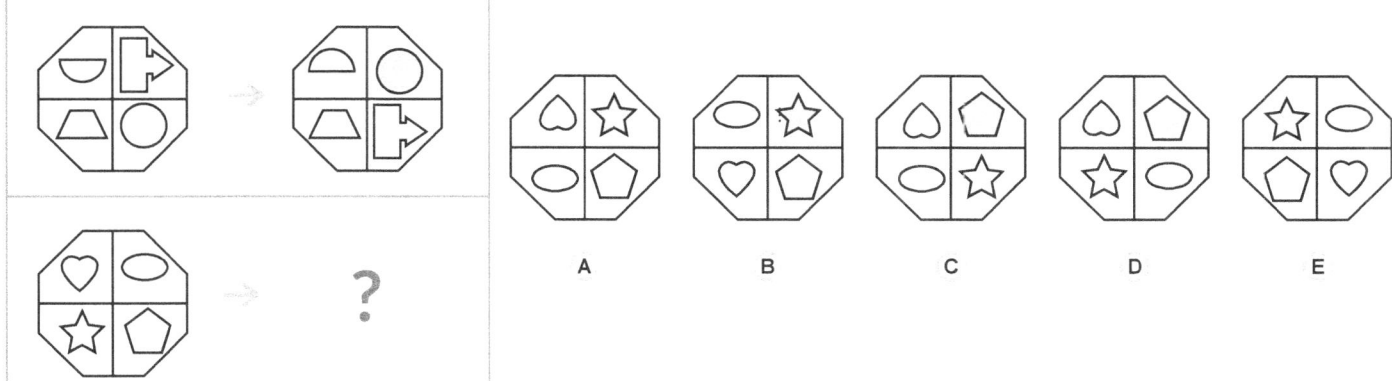

15

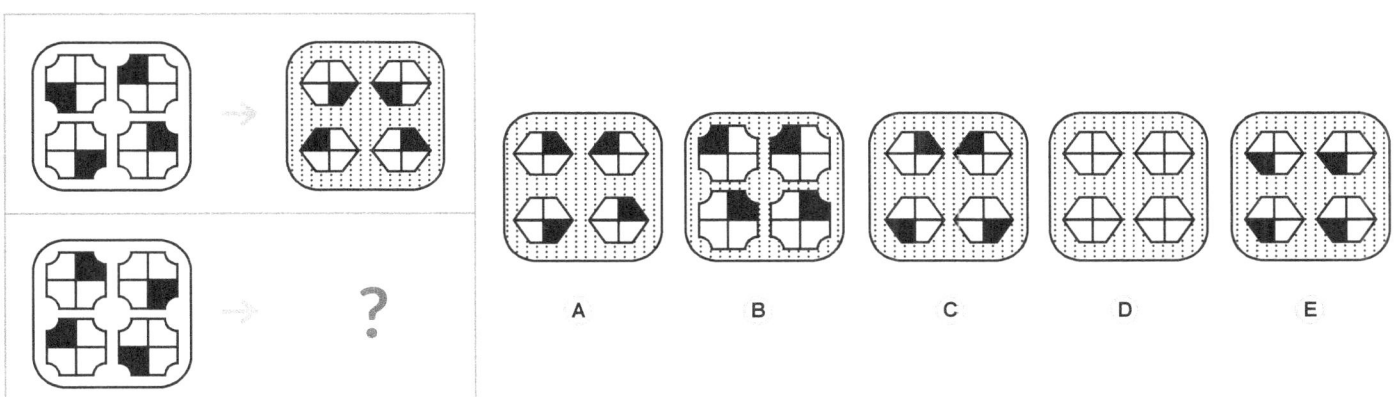

16

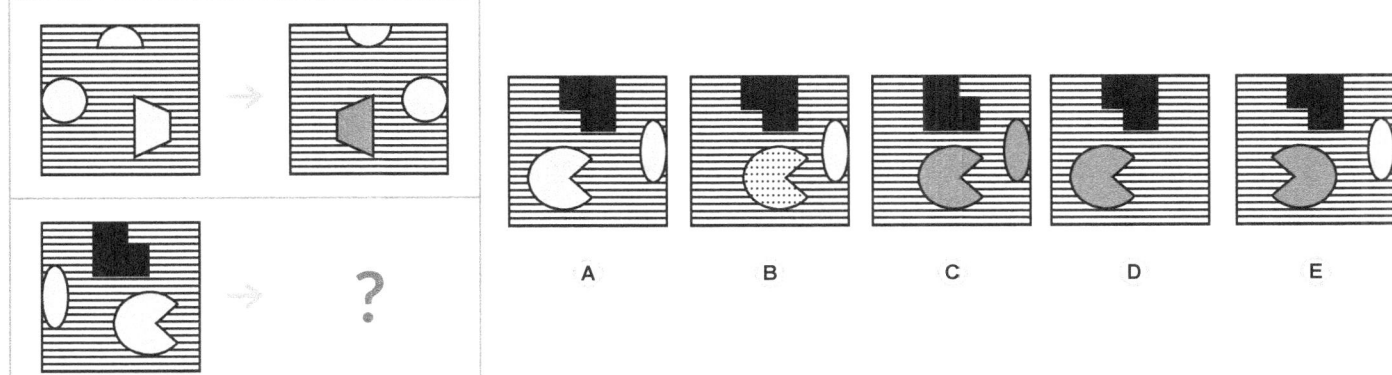

17

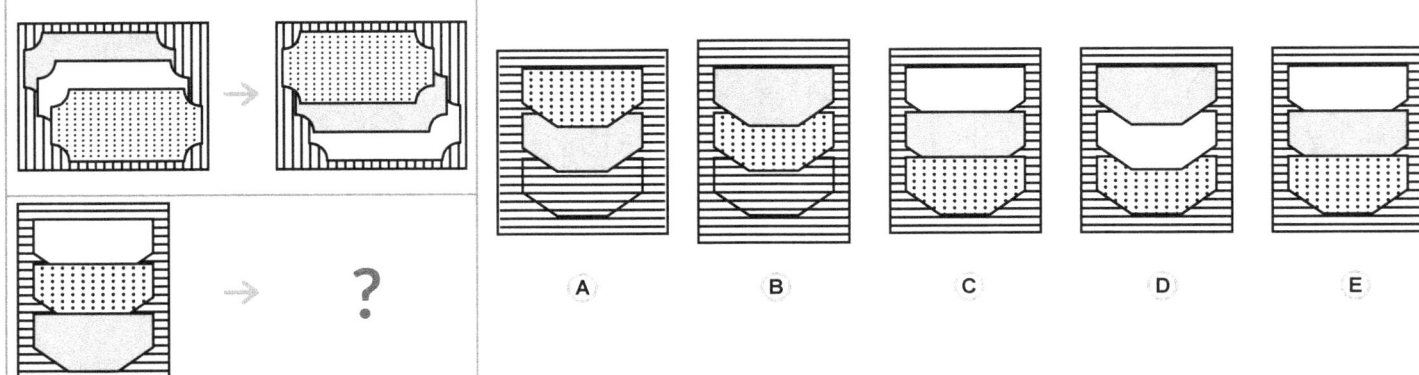

18

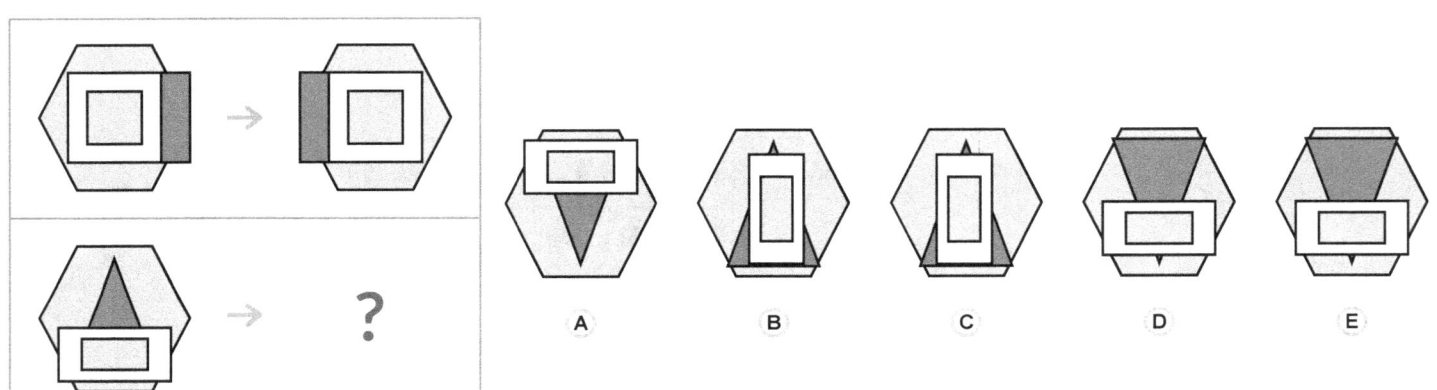

19

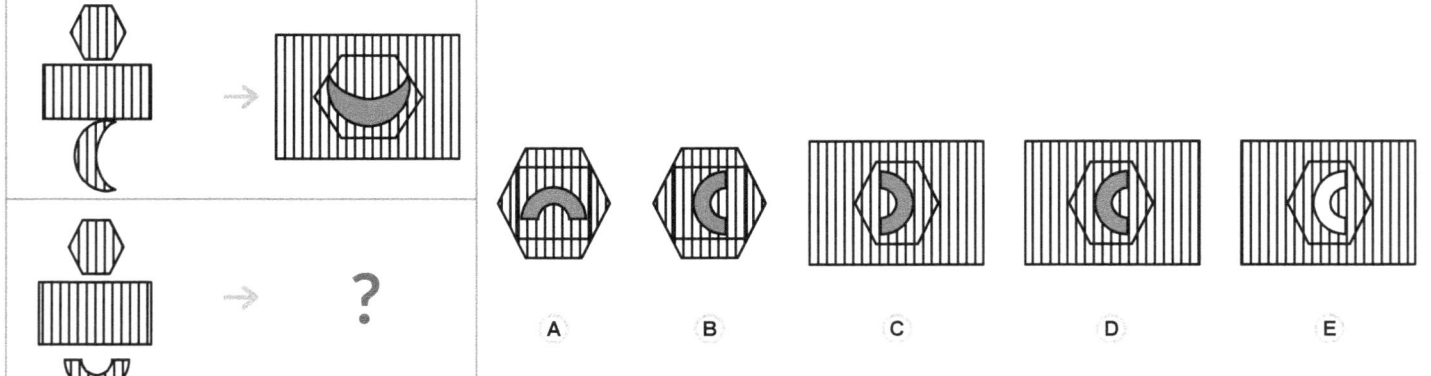

PAPER FOLDING

Directions: The top row of pictures shows a sheet of paper, how it was folded, and then how holes were made in it. Which picture on the bottom row shows how the paper would look after it is unfolded?

Note: To better understand the Paper Folding exercises, you may wish to use real paper and a hole puncher (or scissors). Be sure to notice:

- the number of times the paper is folded (for example, beginning with #3, some questions show paper folded more than once)

- the hole placement

- the number of holes made in the paper

1

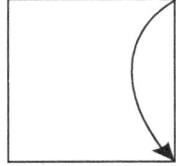 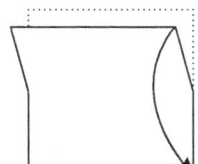 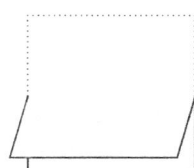 

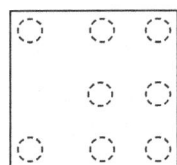 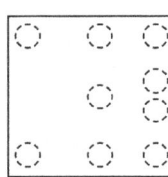 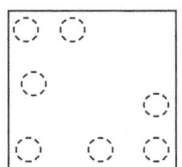 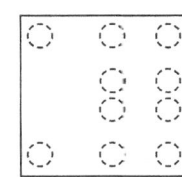 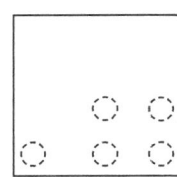

(A) (B) (C) (D) (E)

2

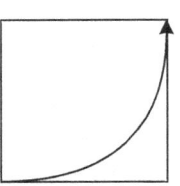 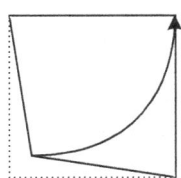 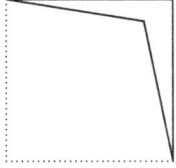 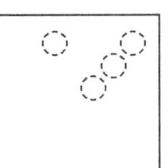

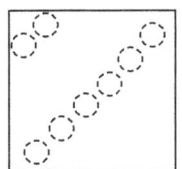 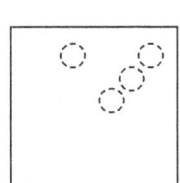 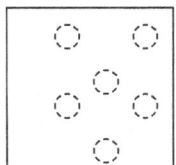 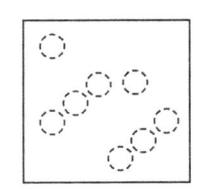 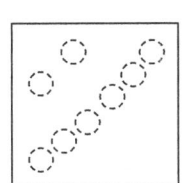

(A) (B) (C) (D) (E)

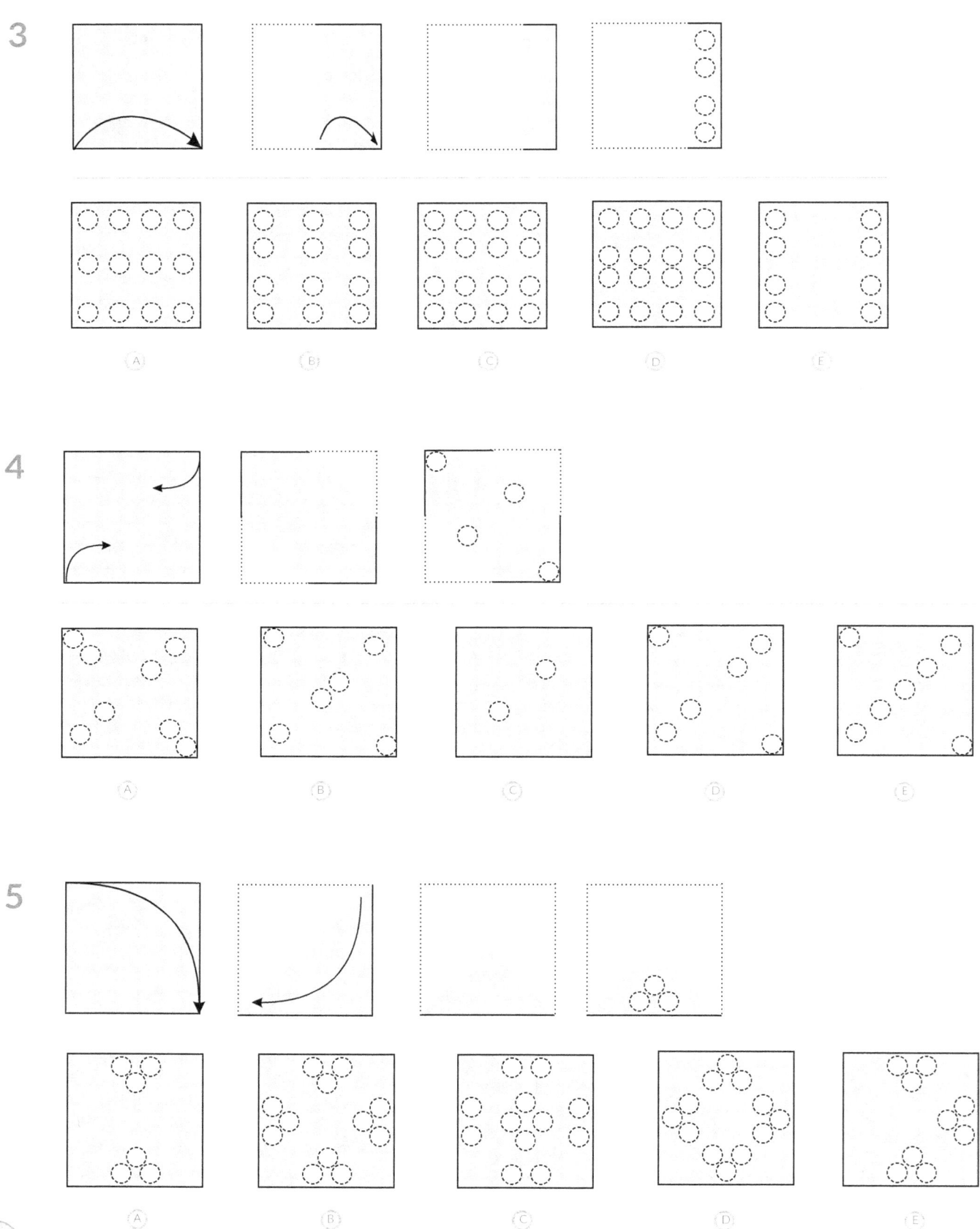

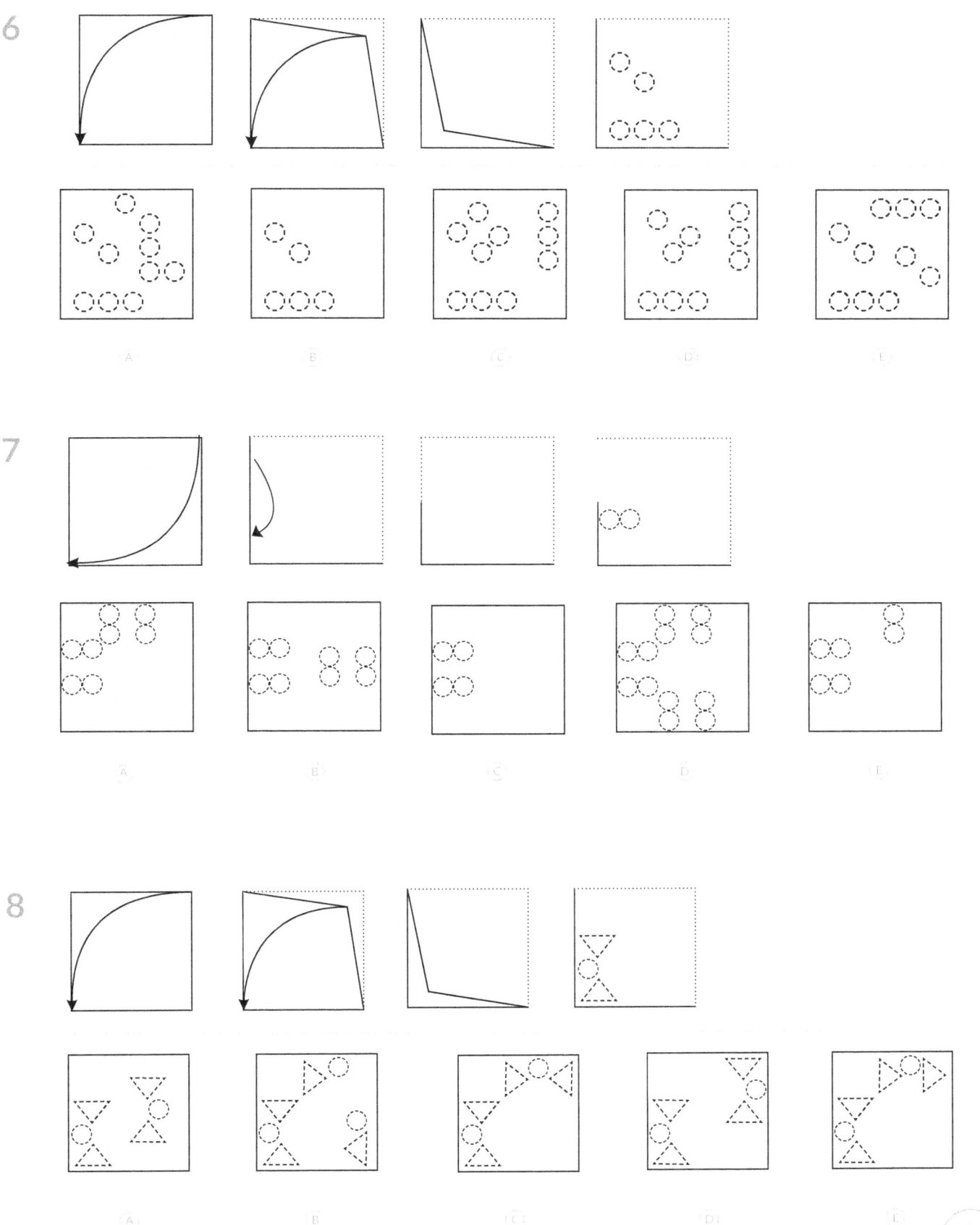

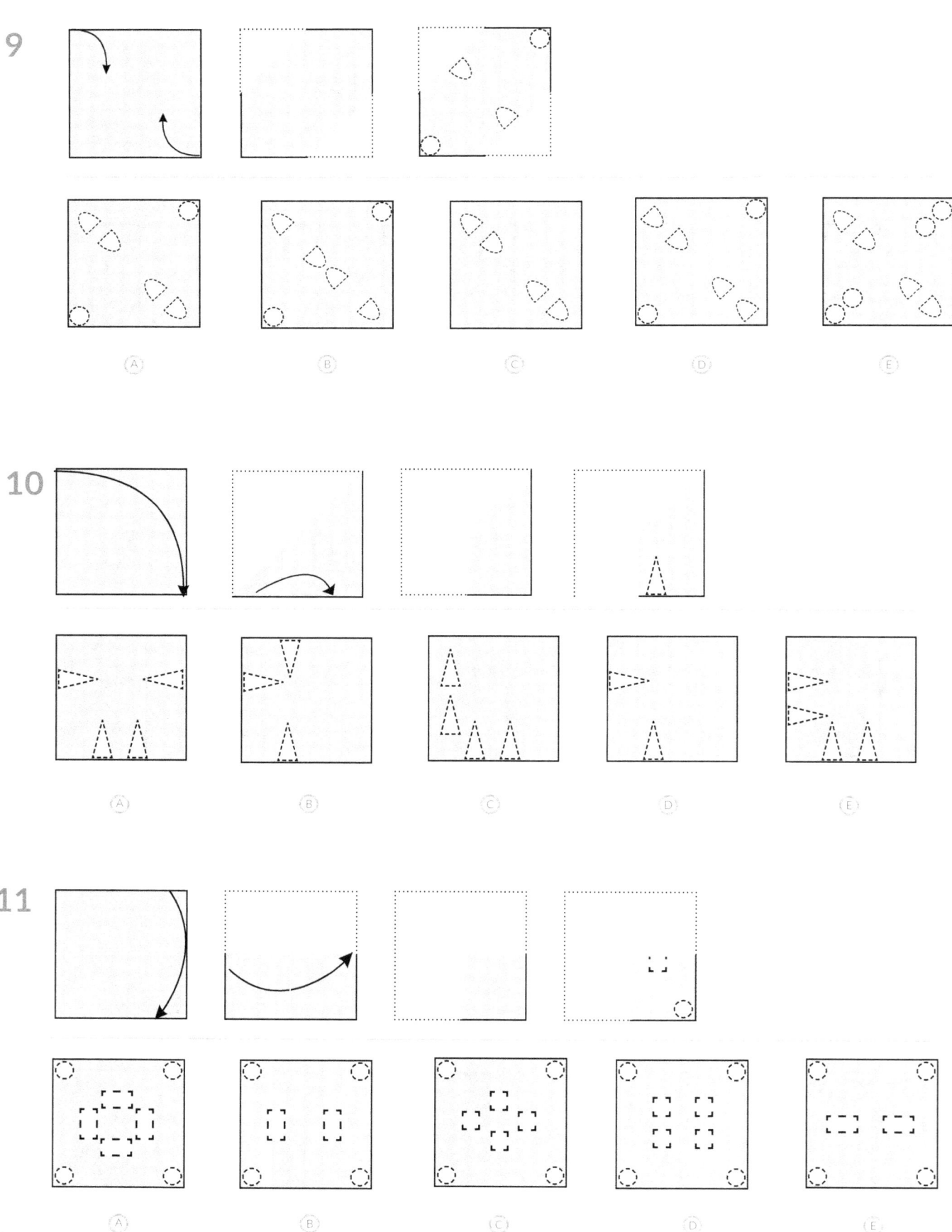

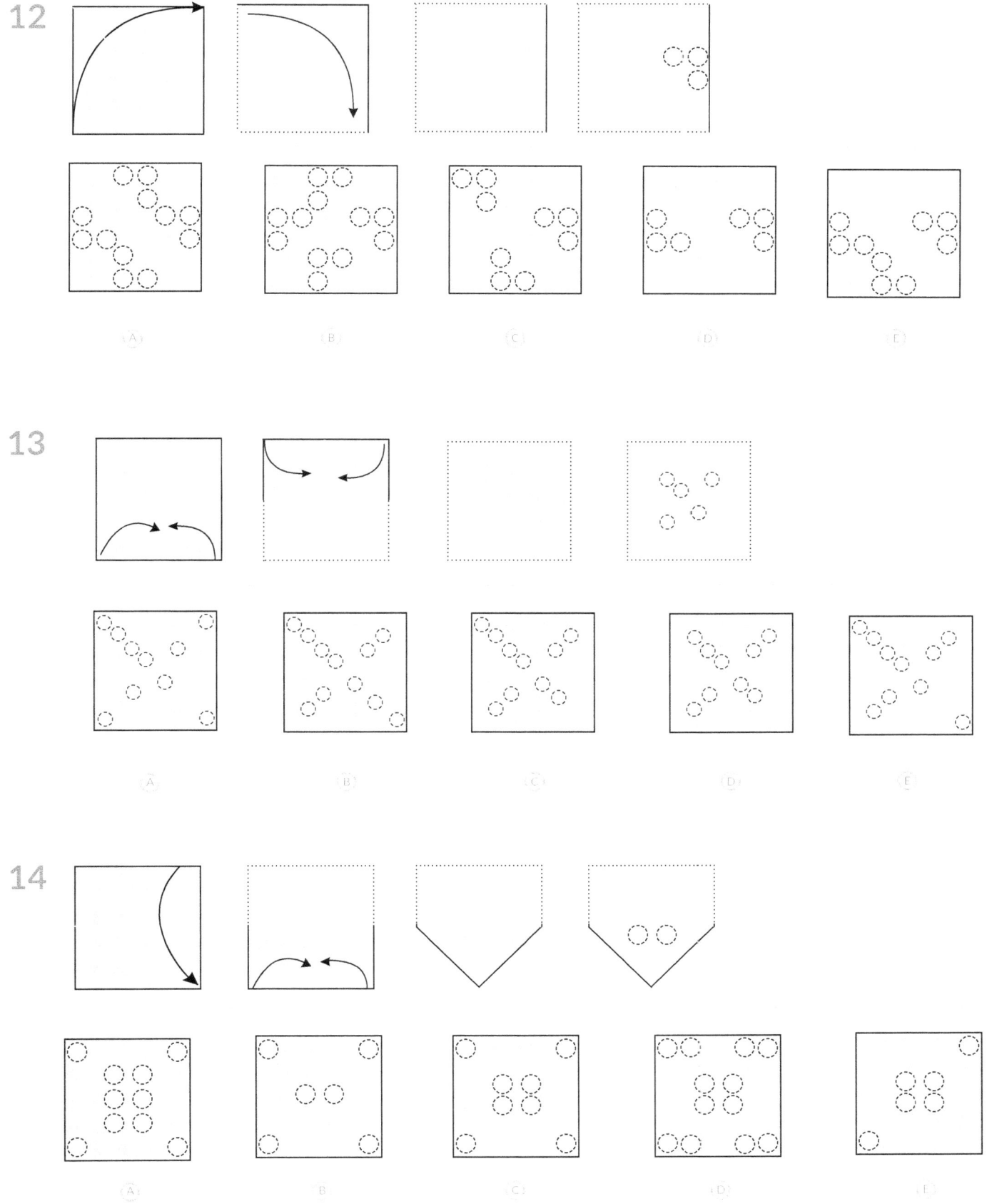

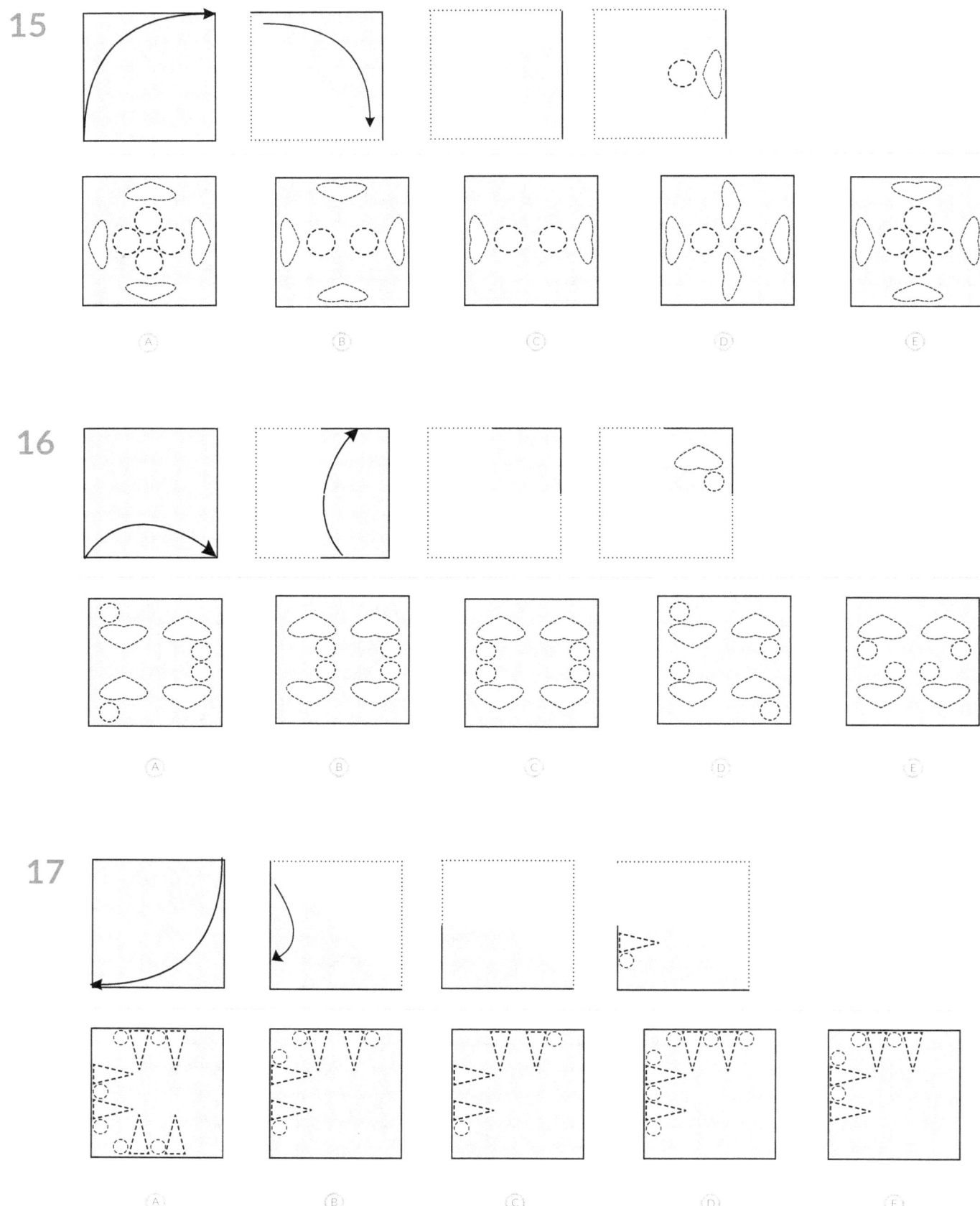

15

16

17

NUMBER PUZZLES

Directions: What answer choice should you put in the place of the question mark so that both sides of the equal sign total the same amount?

Note: As with math problems commonly seen in school, pay close attention to the signs. Do not make the simple mistake of performing the wrong operation (i.e., adding when you should actually be subtracting). Some questions have different operations (i.e., subtracting and division).

Double check your work by replacing the question mark with your answer.

• If you haven't read the Number Puzzles examples on page 9, do so now.

Example 1:

The right side of the equal sign has 149. Which answer choice do you need to put in the place of the question mark so that the left side of the equal sign is also 149? We must add 23.5 to 149. We get 172.5. 172.5 - 23.5 = 149.

So, the answer is 172.5. Answer B is correct.

1   **? - 23.5 = 149**

    A) 125.5   B) 172.5   C) 150   D) 123.5   E) 169.4

2   **84 = 12 × ?**

    A) 5   B) 6   C) 7   D) 10.5   E) 72

3   **5 + 0.75 = 5 + ?/4**

    A) 1   B) 2   C) 3   D) 4   E) 5

4 $5 + 0.6 = ?/5$

   (A) 22   (B) 23   (C) 24   (D) 26   (E) 28

5 $? \div \blacksquare = 25$
$\blacksquare = 16$

   (A) 400   (B) 41   (C) 375   (D) 32   (E) 9

6 $? \div \blacksquare = 12.5$
$\blacksquare = 8.4$

   (A) 10.5   (B) 20.9   (C) 1.488   (D) 97.5   (E) 105

7 $? \div \blacksquare = 72$
$15 - \blacksquare = 9$

   (A) 78   (B) 66   (C) 15   (D) 432   (E) 5

8 $\blacksquare - 5 = ? \times 2$
$\blacksquare = 14 \div 2$

   (A) 4   (B) 2   (C) 3   (D) 1   (E) 6

9   ■ - 3.5 = ? × 1.5
     ■ = 9.6 ÷ 1.2

   Ⓐ 4   Ⓑ 3   Ⓒ 2   Ⓓ 1   Ⓔ 5

10   ■ - (-3) = ? × 2
     ■ = -16 ÷ 2

   Ⓐ -2.5   Ⓑ 2.5   Ⓒ -3   Ⓓ 3   Ⓔ -1

11   ? - ■ = 75
     35 - ■ = 12 + 11

   Ⓐ 92   Ⓑ 87   Ⓒ 70   Ⓓ 83   Ⓔ 96

12   ? = 1/2 + ■
     ■ = 2/5 × 3/4

   Ⓐ 11/20   Ⓑ 13/20   Ⓒ 4/5   Ⓓ 9/20   Ⓔ 5/8

13   ■ ÷ 2 = ?
     ■ = 6 + ●
     ● = 9 - 5

   Ⓐ 4   Ⓑ 2   Ⓒ 7.5   Ⓓ 3   Ⓔ 5

14. $\blacksquare \div 6 = ?$
    $\blacksquare = 32 + \bullet$
    $\bullet = 40 - 18$

    (A) 8   (B) 10   (C) 7   (D) 9   (E) 6

15. $\blacksquare \div 2.5 = ?$
    $\blacksquare = 10.5 + \bullet$
    $\bullet = 6.5 - 2.5$

    (A) 7.8   (B) 5.8   (C) 22   (D) 21   (E) 20

16. $\bullet \div 5 = ?$
    $\bullet = 20 + \blacksquare$
    $\blacksquare = 7 \times 4$

    (A) 6.2   (B) -1.6   (C) 9.6   (D) 10.6   (E) 11.6

17. $\bullet \div 4 = ?$
    $\bullet = 10.5 + \blacksquare$
    $\blacksquare = 5.5 \times 2$

    (A) 4.5   (B) 4.375   (C) 8   (D) 56   (E) 5.375

18. $\bullet \div 1/2 = ?$
    $\bullet = 5 + \blacksquare$
    $\blacksquare = 3/4 \times 8$

    (A) 22   (B) 8   (C) 16   (D) 10   (E) 12

NUMBER ANALOGIES

Directions Look at the first two sets of numbers. Come up with a rule that both of these sets follow. Take this rule to figure out which answer choice goes in the place of the question mark.

Note: As with Verbal Analogies, your child must try to come up with a "rule" to answer the question. It must work with *all* the pairs. Be sure to test it on each one. The "rule" will involve standard math operations (subtraction, addition, division, or multiplication).

Also, the more challenging questions will involve *two operations*.

With all of the Number Analogies questions (as with all questions), it is very important to double check your work to ensure each number pair (and then the answer) follows the rule.

• If you haven't read the Number Analogies examples on page 9, do so now.
• If you need some help with the Number Analogies, #1-#3 (where you use only 1 operation) and #10-#12 (where you must use 2 operations), see the "hints" page on page 10.

Example #1: In the first two sets, you have 5 and 60, 7 and 84. How would you get from 5 to 60? How would you get from 7 to 84? In each set, you must multiply by 12. This is the "rule". Take this rule, look at the number at the beginning of the third set (9) and apply it to the bottom row of answer choices. What is the answer when you multiply 9 x 12? The answer is 108.

1   **[5 → 60]**   **[7 → 84]**   **[9 → ?]**

         96   108   86   12   64

2   **[45 → 3]**   **[75 → 5]**   **[90 → ?]**

         48   20   6   7   15

3   **[12 → 144]**   **[15 → 225]**   **[17 → ?]**

         254   324   272   307   289

4   [2.4 → 0.24]   [5.8 → 0.58]   [7.9 → ?]

   ○ 0.79   ○ 0.079   ○ 0.80   ○ 10.0   ○ 2.68

5   [0.75 → 3/4]   [0.2 → 1/5]   [0.6 → ?]

   ○ 2/3   ○ 1/2   ○ 1/6   ○ 3/5   ○ 5/8

6   [3 → 7]   [5 → 11]   [8 → ?]

   ○ 15   ○ 16   ○ 17   ○ 18   ○ 19

7   [10 → 29]   [15 → 44]   [21 → ?]

   ○ 60   ○ 62   ○ 64   ○ 65   ○ 66

8   [4 → 17]   [7 → 50]   [9 → ?]

   ○ 80   ○ 81   ○ 82   ○ 83   ○ 84

9   [50 → 26]   [90 → 46]   [64 → ?]

  ○ 36   ○ 35   ○ 34   ○ 33   ○ 32

10   [40 → 13]   [56 → 17]   [72 → ?]

  ○ 18   ○ 15   ○ 20   ○ 27   ○ 21

11   [5 → 19]   [7 → 25]   [9 → ?]

  ○ 31   ○ 30   ○ 29   ○ 28   ○ 27

12   [2 → 8]   [3 → 27]   [5 → ?]

  ○ 15   ○ 50   ○ 100   ○ 125   ○ 150

13   [3 → 26]   [4 → 63]   [5 → ?]

  ○ 124   ○ 125   ○ 126   ○ 127   ○ 128

14 [6 → 25] [8 → 33] [10 → ?]

○ 37 ○ 41 ○ 39 ○ 43 ○ 25

15 [4 → 13] [6 → 33] [8 → ?]

○ 61 ○ 62 ○ 63 ○ 64 ○ 65

16 [12 → 4] [20 → 6] [9 → ?]

○ 2.5 ○ 3.5 ○ 3.75 ○ 4.5 ○ 3.25

17 [1.5 → 2.25] [2.3 → 5.29] [3.6 → ?]

○ 10.96 ○ 11.56 ○ 12.24 ○ 12.96 ○ 13.21

18 [5 → 2.25] [9 → 3.25] [12 → ?]

○ 3.5 ○ 3.75 ○ 4 ○ 4.25 ○ 4.5

NUMBER SERIES

Directions: Here, you must try to figure out a pattern that the numbers have made. Which answer choice would complete the pattern?

Note: As with other question types, it is helpful to figure out a "rule" that the numbers have made. In this section, it is a pattern. Use the "rule"/pattern to figure out the missing number. As with the Number Analogies, the rules will involve subtraction, addition, division, or multiplication.

Some of these are quite challenging and involve more than one "rule". They could even involve more than one kind of operation (addition/subtraction/multiplication/division).

Double check your work to ensure the series of numbers (and then the answer) follows the rule/pattern.

- If you haven't read the Number Series examples on page 9, do so now.
- If you need some help with the Number Series, #1-#3 (where you use only 1 operation) and #8-#10 (where you must use 2 operations), see the "hints" page on page 10.

Example #1: Do you see a pattern or a rule that the numbers in the series follow? How do you get from 4 to 12, then from 12 to 36, then from 36 to 108? Each time, each number is multiplied by 3. If this is the pattern, then what would come after 108? It's Choice D, 324.

1   **4**   **12**   **36**   **108**   **?**

   ○ 138   ○ 111   ○ 432   ○ 324   ○ 336

2   **45.5**   **16.5**   **-12.5**   **-41.5**   **?**

   ○ 29.5   ○ 30.5   ○ -29   ○ 70.5   ○ -70.5

3 29   60   29   65   29   70   29 ?

○ 29   ○ 75   ○ 72   ○ 80   ○ 34

4 15   14   12   11   9   ?

○ 6   ○ 5   ○ 4   ○ 7   ○ 8

5 3.5   4.5   6.5   7.5   9.5   ?

○ 10.5   ○ 10.0   ○ 10.05   ○ 11.5   ○ 12.5

6 150   129   107   84   60   ?

○ 34   ○ 36   ○ 35   ○ 33   ○ 48

7 2.5 3.5   4.5   6.5   7.5 8.5   10.5   ?

○ 9.5   ○ 11.5   ○ 12.5   ○ 10.0   ○ 13.0

8   5   10   30   120   ?

○ 240   ○ 360   ○ 480   ○ 600   ○ 720

9   44   56   44   28   44   14   44   ?

○ 44   ○ 10   ○ 12   ○ 7   ○ 8

10   32   33   34   36   37   38   40   41   ?

○ 42   ○ 44   ○ 43   ○ 45   ○ 46

11   5   10   11   22   23   ?

○ 44   ○ 45   ○ 46   ○ 47   ○ 48

12   5   20   10   40   20   ?

○ 10   ○ 100   ○ 40   ○ 120   ○ 80

13 5 13 10 17 25 22 ?

- 30
- 29
- 31
- 33
- 32

14 34 19 35 20 36 21 37 22 ?

- 23
- 24
- 38
- 39
- 25

15 40 10 38 12 36 14 34 16 ?

- 32
- 18
- 20
- 30
- 22

16 8 10 12 11 13 15 14 16 ?

- 13
- 15
- 16
- 17
- 18

17 5 6 7 6 8 10 8 11 14 ?

- 10
- 13
- 12
- 11
- 15

18   **3**   **6**   **12**   **6**   **12**   **24**   **12**   **24**   **48**   **?**

○ 96   ○ 24   ○ 12   ○ 48   ○ 36

19   **20**   **23**   **27**   **32**   **38**   **45**   **53**   **?**

○ 60   ○ 62   ○ 61   ○ 63   ○ 65

20   **15**   **9**   **14**   **10**   **13**   **11**   **?**

○ 10   ○ 9   ○ 12   ○ 7   ○ 15

- End of Practice Test 1. Practice Test 2 begins on the next page. -

1   **lynx**   **leopard**   **ocelot**

(A) aardvark   (B) viper   (C) panther   (D) beluga   (E) falcon

2   **limousine**   **funicular**   **gondola**

(A) jet ski   (B) tanker truck   (C) dump truck   (D) tractor trailer   (E) cargo ship

3   **zoologist**   **microbiologist**   **ecologist**

(A) geologist   (B) botanist   (C) astronomer   (D) chemist   (E) minerologist

4   **enhance**   **refine**   **renovate**

(A) neglect   (B) degenerate   (C) deteriorate   (D) amend   (E) impair

5   **trench**   **trough**   **abyss**

(A) crest   (B) height   (C) elevation   (D) peak   (E) valley

6   **canopy**   **awning**   **umbrella**

(A) tarp   (B) lamp   (C) window   (D) vase   (E) shovel

7   **driving**   **knitting**   **coding**

(A) speaking   (B) walking   (C) eating   (D) woodworking   (E) sleeping

8   **silo**   **vault**   **cellar**

(A) stool   (B) mantle   (C) sculpture   (D) display   (E) warehouse

9   **saunter**   **dart**   **ascend**

(A) contemplate   (B) recline   (C) meander   (D) articulate   (E) envision

10 dissolution   fragmentation   severance

A coalition   B competition   C division   D conjunction   E fusion

11 scant   minimal   meager

A finite   B abundant   C plethora   D multitude   E innumerable

12 pedestal   easel   mannequin

A drawer   B showcase   C cabinet   D barrel   E basket

13 hibernate   hover   dwell

A traverse   B depart   C saunter   D stagnate   E vault

14 channel   fjord   reservoir

A bluff   B canyon   C plateau   D mirage   E strait

15 catalog   flyer   manuscript

A canvas   B pamphlet   C easel   D broadcast   E hologram

16 compute   deduce   quantify

A speculate   B consolidate   C tabulate   D fabricate   E accumulate

17 accolade   certificate   plaque

A memo   B journal   C poster   D honor   E announcement

18 mollusk   vertebrate   bacteria

A crystal   B fungus   C mineral   D polymer   E circuit

19 migrate   evacuate   circumnavigate

A ascend   B contemplate   C ponder   D procrastinate   E transcribe

VERBAL ANALOGIES, PRACTICE TEST 2 / **Directions**: The first set of words goes together in some way. Which answer choice would make the second set of words go together in the same way as the first set?

1   **metal > fragment : bread > ?**

(A) loaf   (B) slice   (C) crust   (D) dough   (E) crumb

2   **artist > occupation : cathedral > ?**

(A) altar   (B) plaza   (C) mansion   (D) monument   (E) sculpture

3   **accumulate > gather : disperse > ?**

(A) collect   (B) scatter   (C) attract   (D) dissolve   (E) compile

4   **glimmer > blaze : murmur > ?**

(A) shout   (B) echo   (C) melody   (D) whisper   (E) text

5   **internet > encyclopedia : GPS > ?**

(A) smartphone   (B) satellite   (C) map   (D) vehicle   (E) highway

6   **malnutrition > health : misinformation > ?**

(A) suspicion   (B) deception   (C) confusion   (D) hunch   (E) accuracy

7   **study > comprehension : practice > ?**

(A) repetition   (B) fatigue   (C) expertise   (D) routine   (E) effort

8   **length > shortened : complexity > ?**

(A) elongated   (B) simplified   (C) perplexed   (D) complicated   (E) combined

9   **apathetic > emotion : silent > ?**

(A) noise   (B) peace   (C) communication   (D) motion   (E) connection

10   **elaborate > complex : momentous > ?**

(A) trivial   (B) negligible   (C) subtle   (D) momentary   (E) significant

11   **atom > molecule : verse > ?**

    A word   B illustration   C table of contents   D poem   E rhyme

12   **editor > revise : translator > ?**

    A restore   B interpret   C suppress   D simplify   E acknowledge

13   **harmony > discord : clarity > ?**

    A confusion   B transparency   C illumination   D brightness   E articulation

14   **chisel > sculpture : scalpel : ?**

    A blade   B hospital   C surgeon   D surgery   E painting

15   **profound > deep : arduous > ?**

    A tedious   B functional   C challenging   D distinct   E monotonous

16   **exorbitant > reasonable : candid > ?**

    A careful   B impartial   C moderate   D thorough   E secretive

17   **innovative > creativity : resolute > ?**

    A determination   B confusion   C uncertainty   D hesitation   E flexibility

18   **adorn > decorate : refute > ?**

    A argue   B confirm   C concede   D disprove   E defend

19   **infallible > error : immutable > ?**

    A mistake   B mute   C change   D delay   E stability

20   **tenacious > persistent : terse> ?**

    A incessant   B concise   C verbose   D vague   E convoluted

1   To ensure accurate results, it is important to use _____ methods for analyzing the data.

(A) random   (B) experimental   (C) precise   (D) inconsistent   (E) optional

2   The students became _____ when they found out they would be getting a new auditorium with modern facilities.

(A) indifferent   (B) enthusiastic   (C) disheartened   (D) apprehensive   (E) lethargic

3   The state's array of _____ parks appeals to those searching for unspoiled wilderness.

(A) urban   (B) cultivated   (C) theme   (D) congested   (E) pristine

4   When picking a book to read, she has a noticeable _____ for mysteries, enjoying the suspense and solving the puzzles.

(A) aversion   (B) fondness   (C) clue   (D) indifference   (E) apathy

5   The sensitive electronics should be kept away from heat to prevent _____.

(A) illumination   (B) protection   (C) insulation   (D) operation   (E) malfunction

6 The new program aims to _____ the growth of eco-friendly farming techniques.

   A extract   B obstruct   C facilitate   D irrigate   E erode

7 Due to the water supply being _____, the residents were forced to depend on bottled water for drinking.

   A contaminated   B filtered   C pristine   D desalinated   E potable

8 The author wrote many _____ novels, each exploring different themes and writing styles.

   A generic   B repetitive   C predictable   D original   E monotonous

9 The new software _____ improved the team's productivity, making their work much more efficient.

   A marginally   B questionably   C dramatically   D insignificantly   E randomly

10 The players became _____ after the championship game was delayed again due to inclement weather.

   A exasperated   B elated   C triumphant   D optimistic   E indifferent

11 When the students presented their science project, the _____ results captivated the judges, which _____ their enthusiasm for the experiment.

A remarkable, heightened   B ambiguous, reduced   C mundane, lessened   D perplexing, diminished   E trivial, diverted

12 To _____ the important details, he used a _____ headline for his final report.

A indicate, plain   B underscore, bold   C block, flashy   D obscure, minimal   E edit, transparent

13 The video game's experience was elevated by the inclusion of _____ quests and characters with _____ traits.

A fascinating, aggravating   B predictable, simple   C common, appealing   D routine, systematic   E captivating, engaging

14 For Lisa to _____ her training goals, it is _____ that she practices regularly.

A achieve, irrelevant   B foster, inconsequential   C implement, trivial   D attain, imperative   E accomplish, optional

15 The researchers _____ at the conference to discuss their findings, considering the gathering a vital _____ for collaboration.

A linger, burden   B disperse, problem   C converge, occasion   D gather, obstacle   E separate, barrier

16   The two _____ approaches to the problem offer _____ outcomes.

A divergent,   B identical,   C predictable,   D interchangeable,   E dubious,
   varied   conflicting   uncertain   different   reliable

17   Designers use bright colors to _____ the _____ of products like candy.

A conceal,   B amplify,   C increase,   D obscure,   E improve,
   flavor   appeal   texture   quality   clarity

18   To ensure a successful city event, the organizers must _____ the budget by
focusing on _____ expenses.

A inflate,   B ignore,   C increase,   D extend,   E control,
   unnecessary   optional   excessive   trivial   essential

19   One challenge with hiking is that it becomes more _____ as you ascend to
higher _____ .

A demanding,   B unpredictable,   C attainable,   D strenuous,   E relaxing,
   depths   troughs   levels   altitudes   ridges

20   To _____ the risk of wildfires, the forest service _____ new fire prevention
measures.

A heighten,   B minimize,   C diminish,   D safeguard,   E extinguish,
   delays   implements   investigates   reviews   analyzes

Figure Classification Directions: Which answer choice in the bottom row goes best with the 3 pictures in the top row?

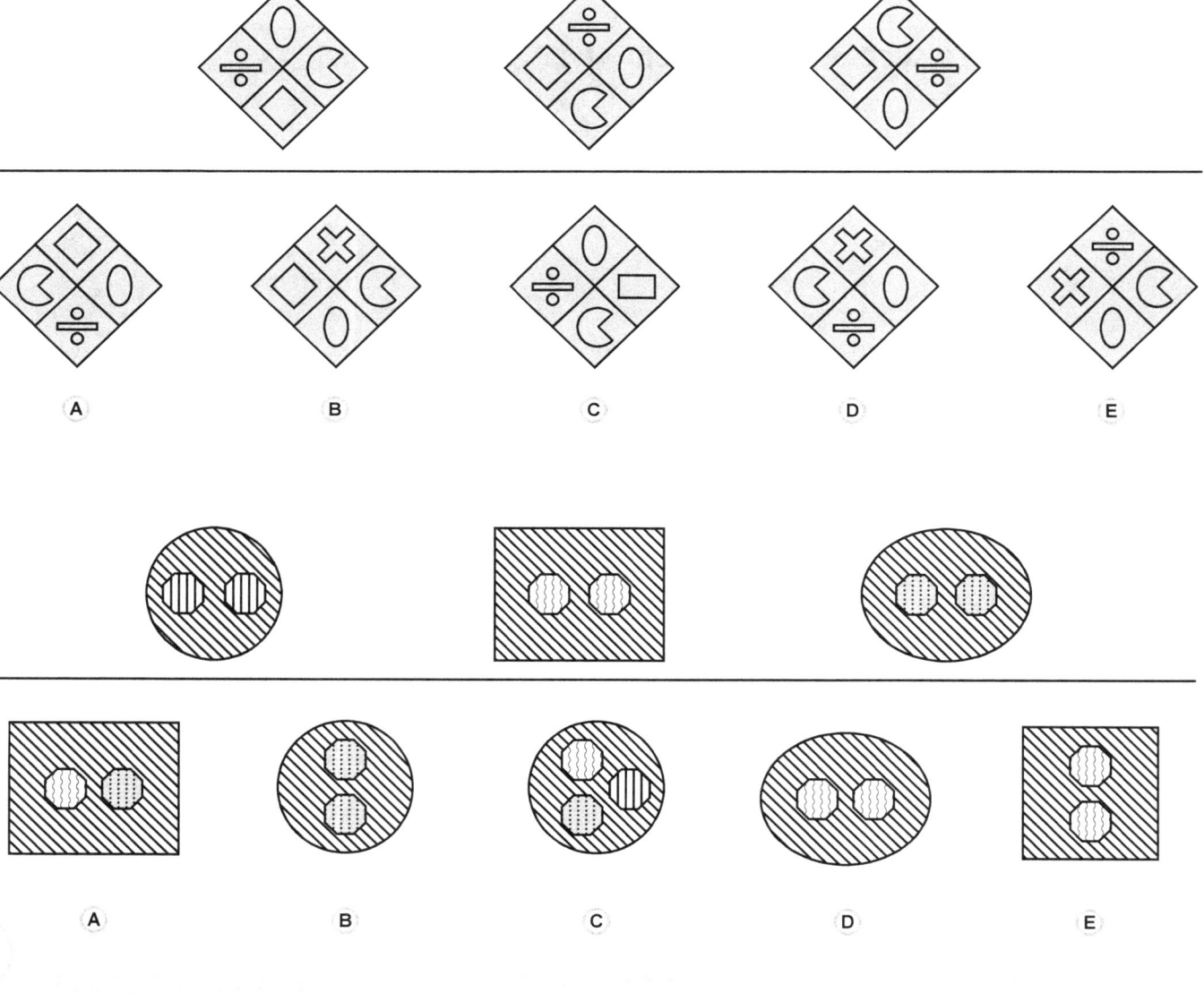

4

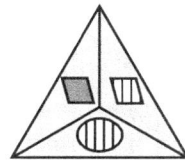 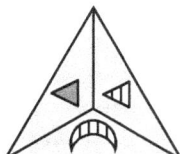 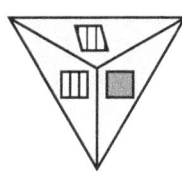

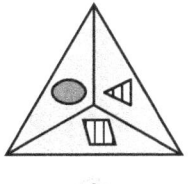 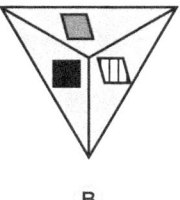 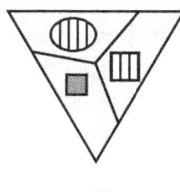 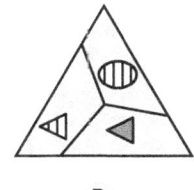 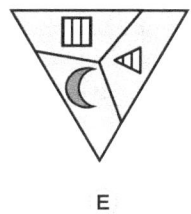

A   B   C   D   E

5

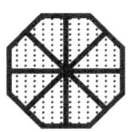 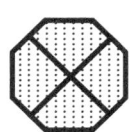 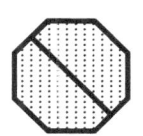

 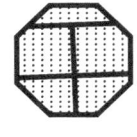   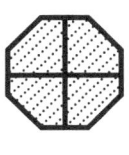

A   B   C   D   E

6

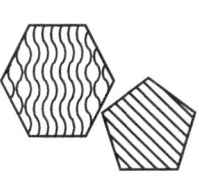  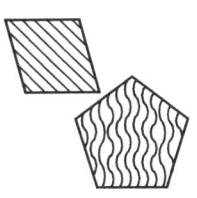

  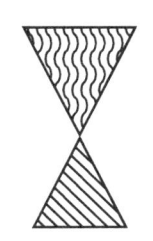  

A   B   C   D   E

7

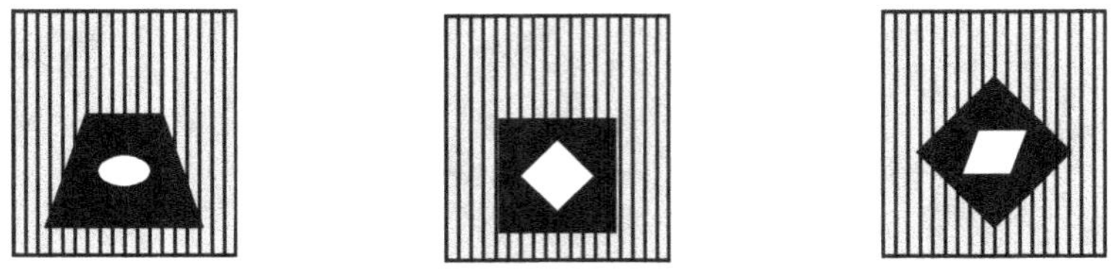

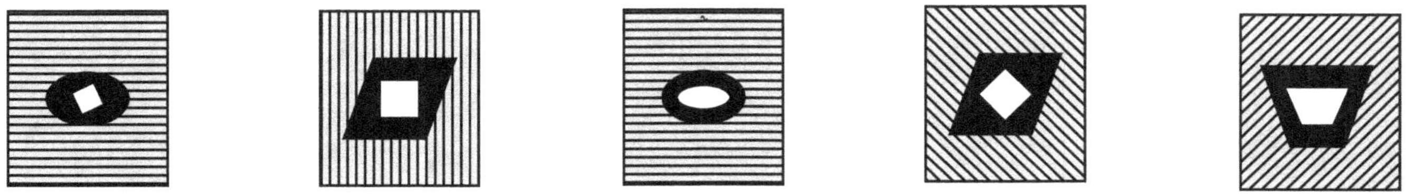

A B C D E

8

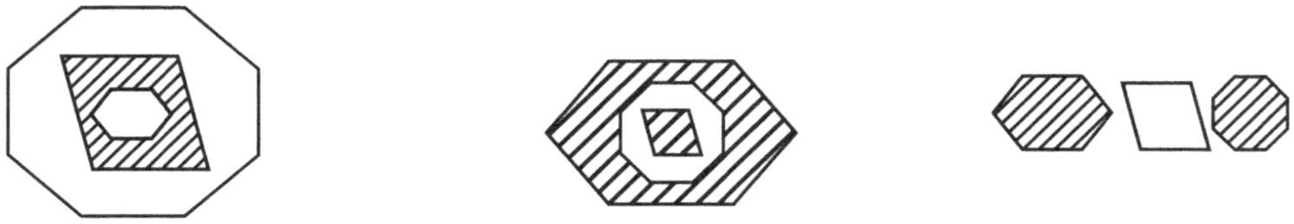

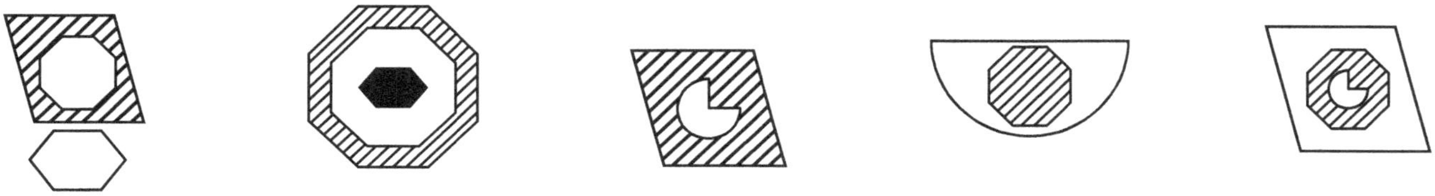

A B C D E

9

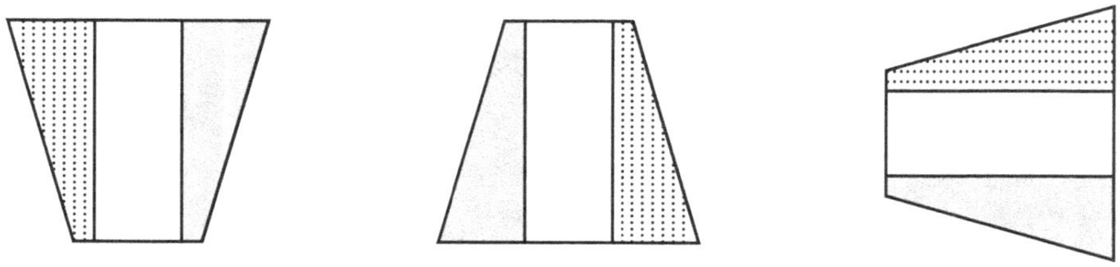

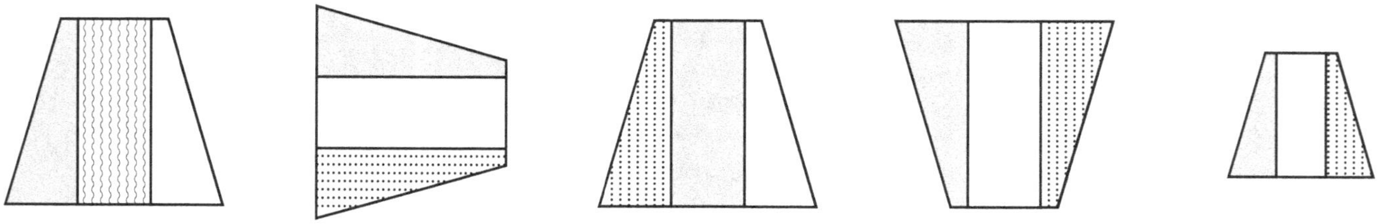

A B C D E

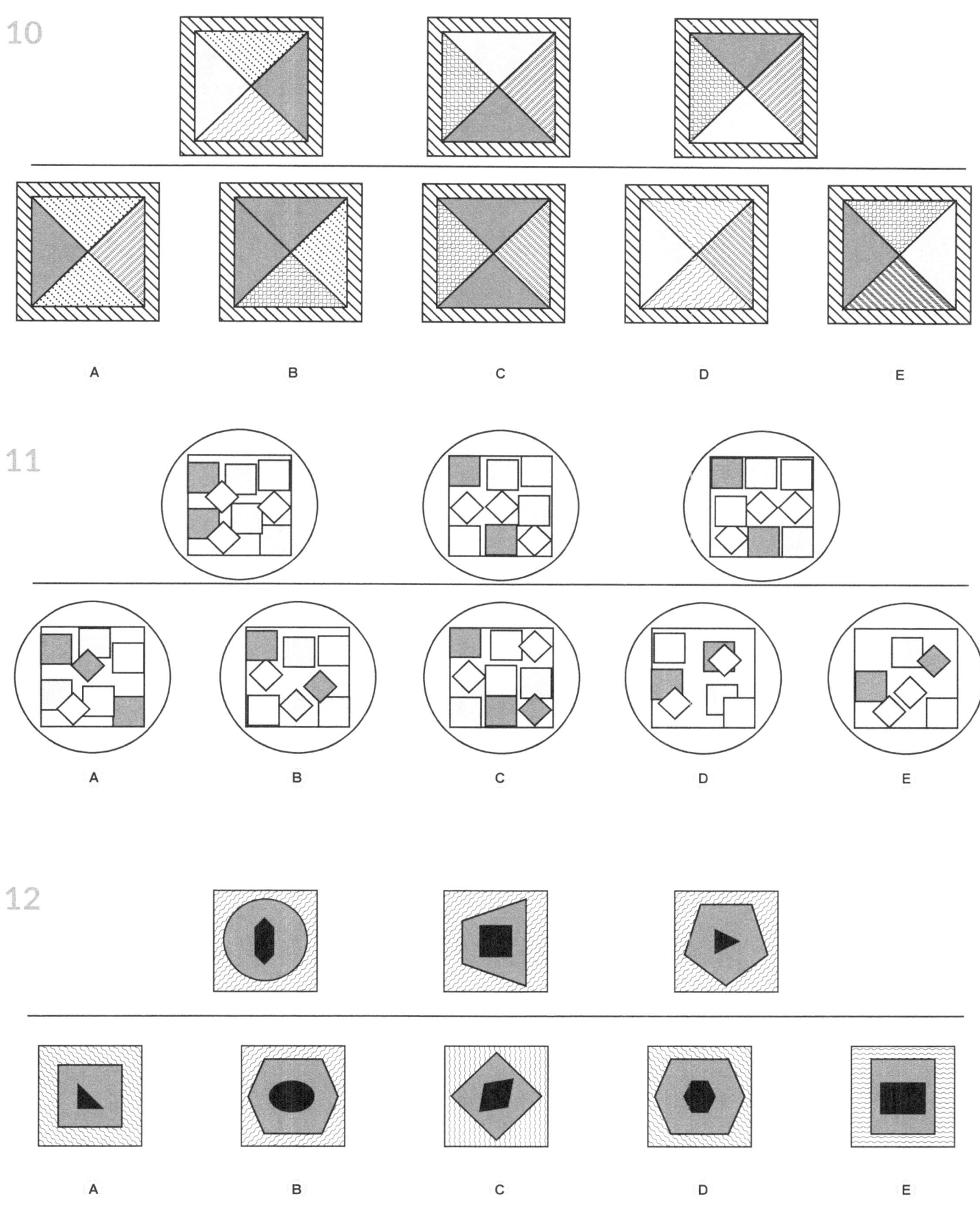

10

11

12

A   B   C   D   E

13

14

15

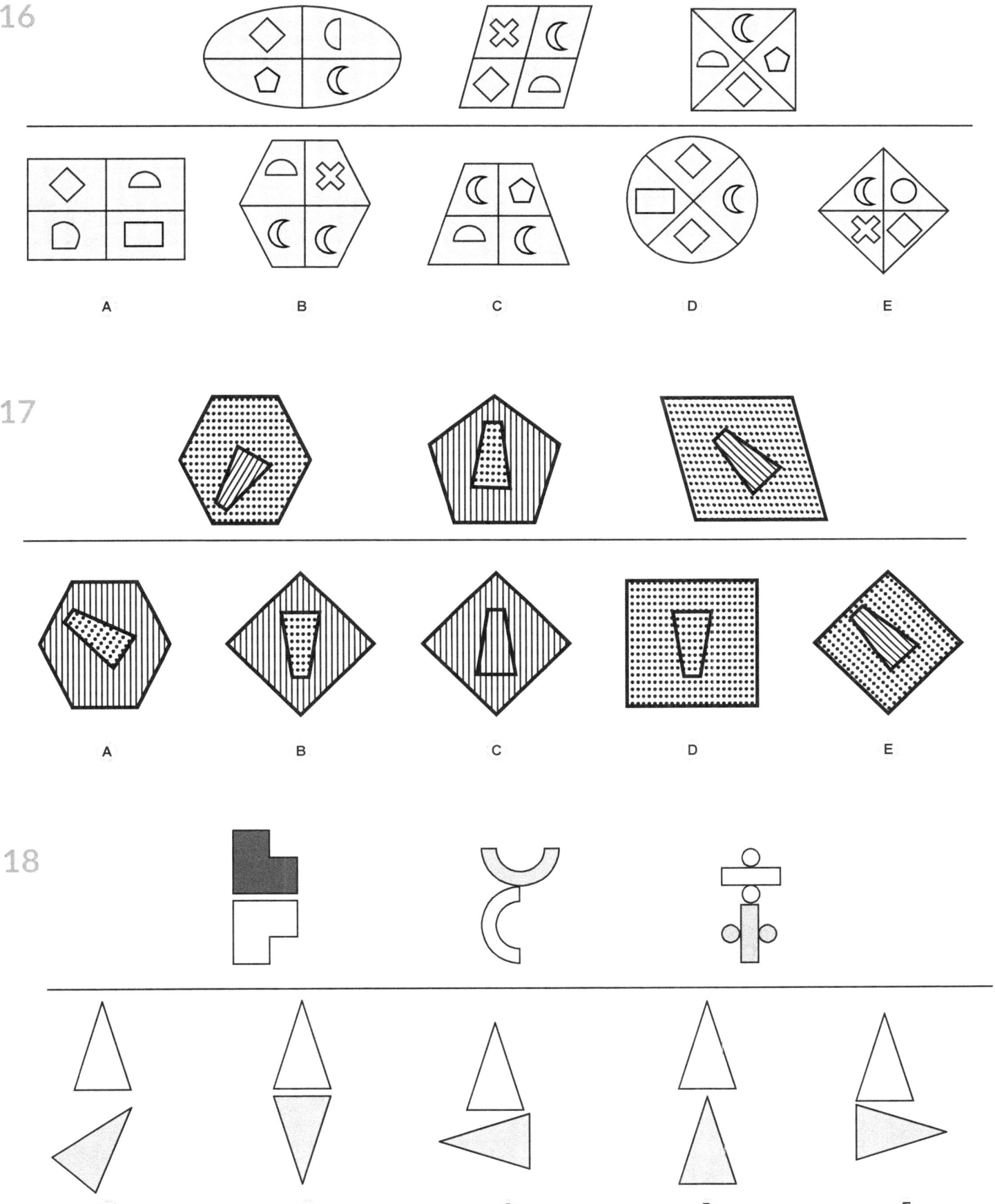

Figure Analogies Directions: Which choice makes the second set of pictures go together in the same way as the first set?

1

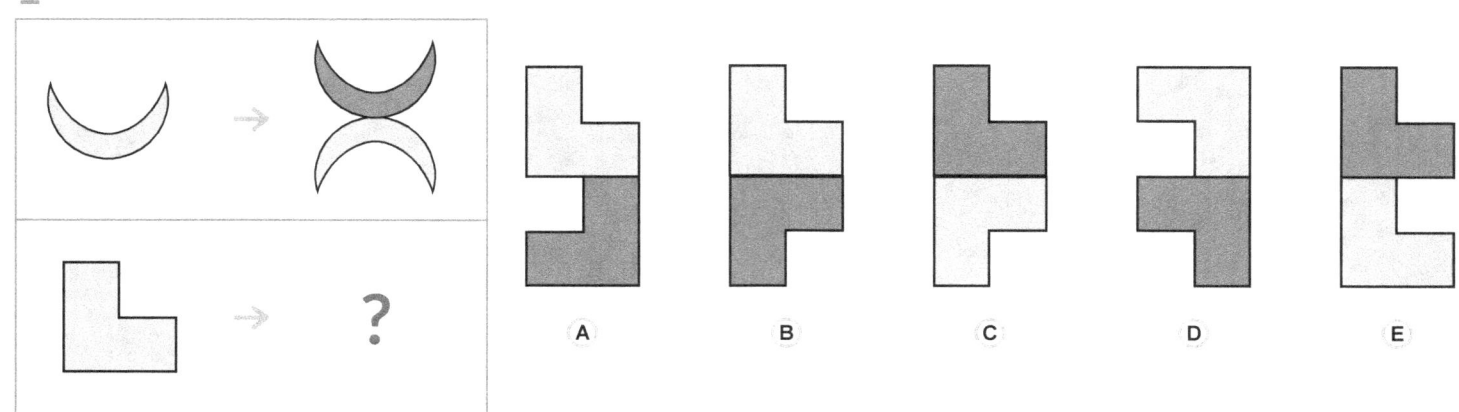

2

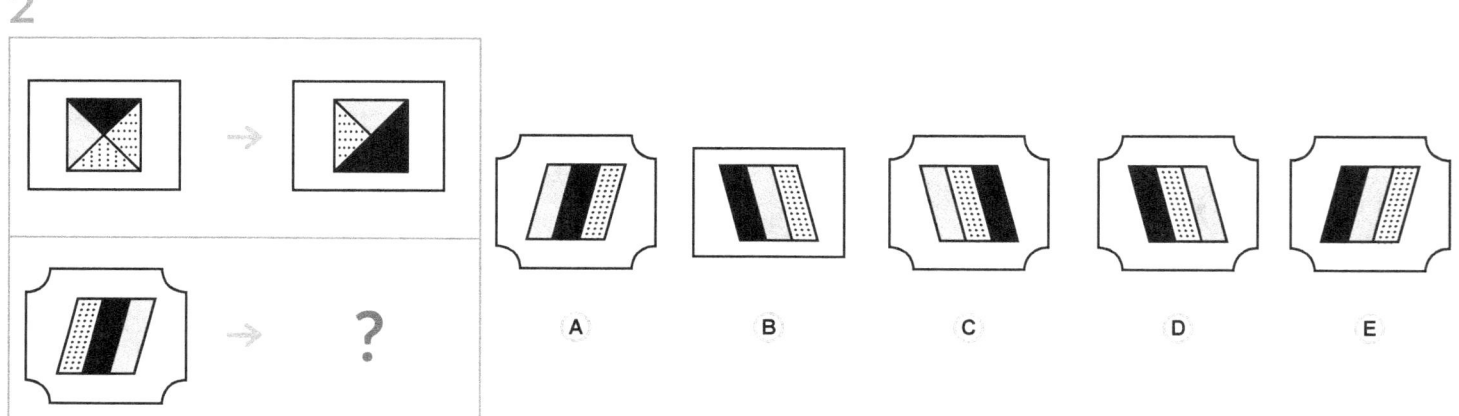

3

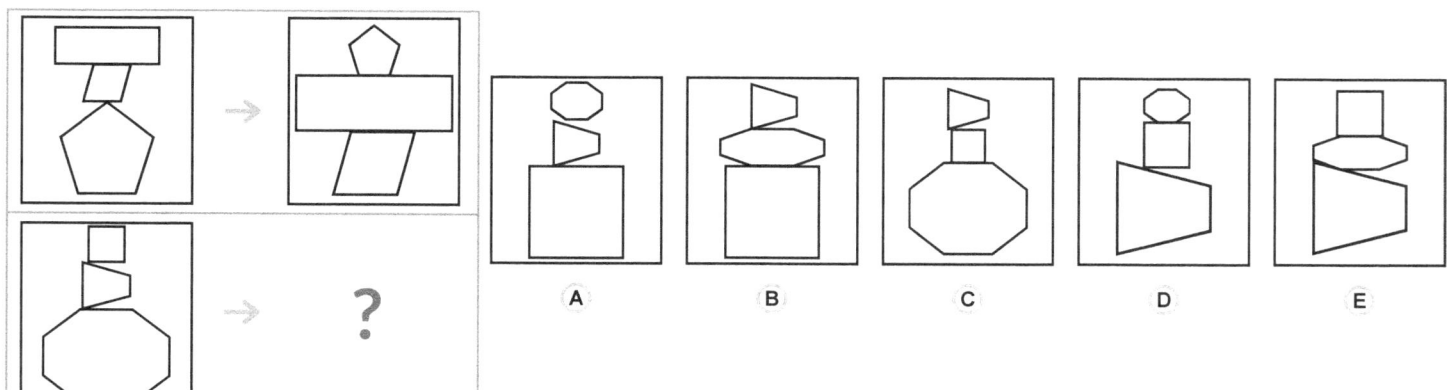

4

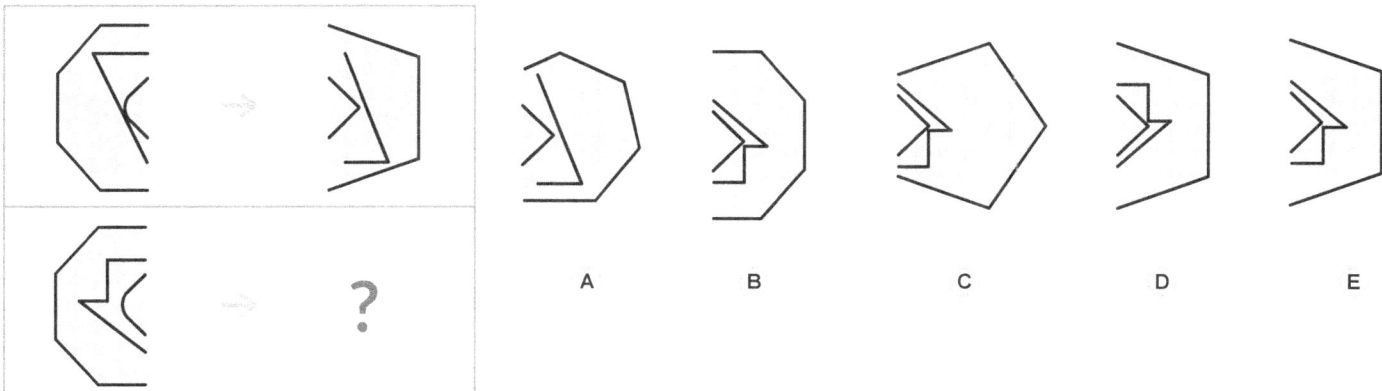

A B C D E

5

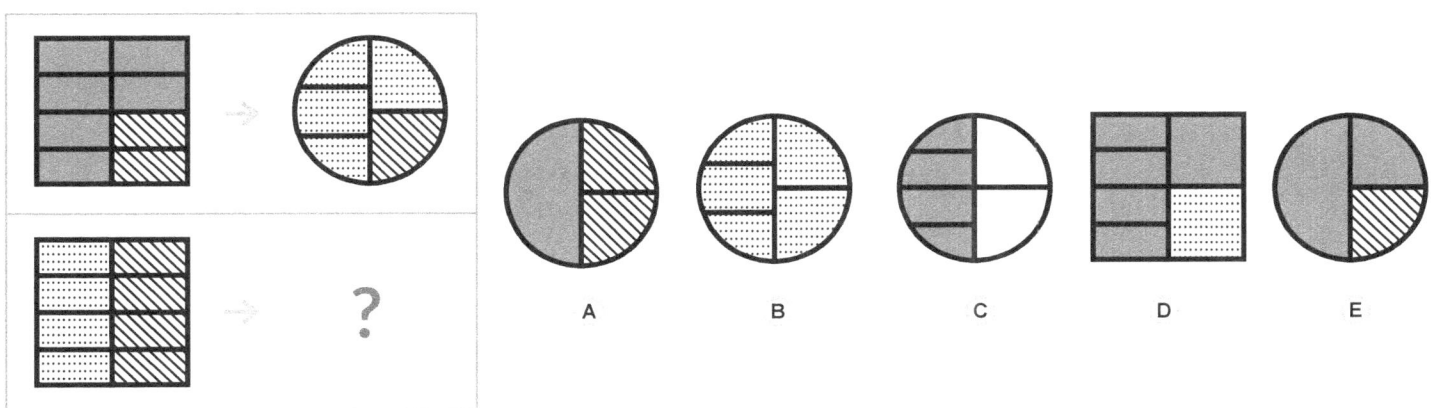

A B C D E

6

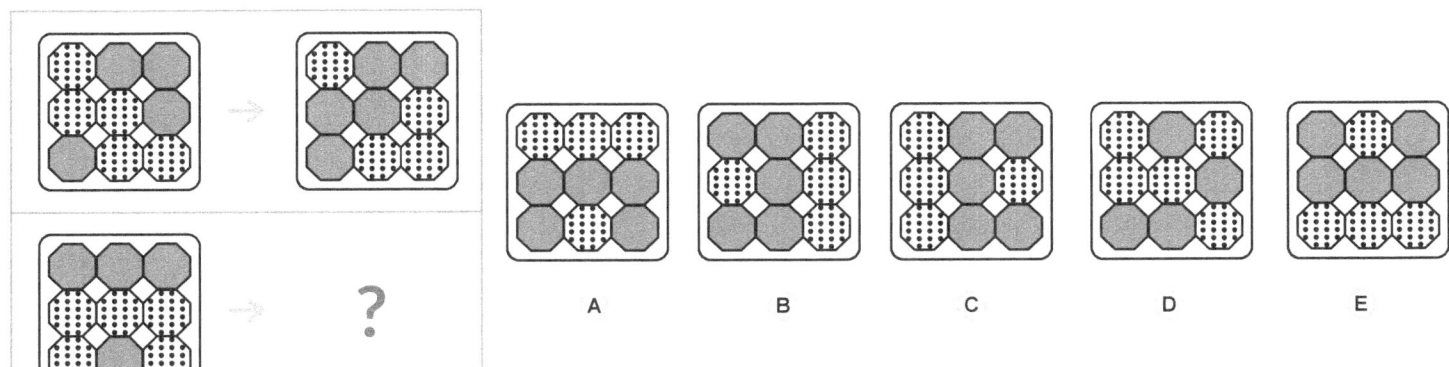

A B C D E

7

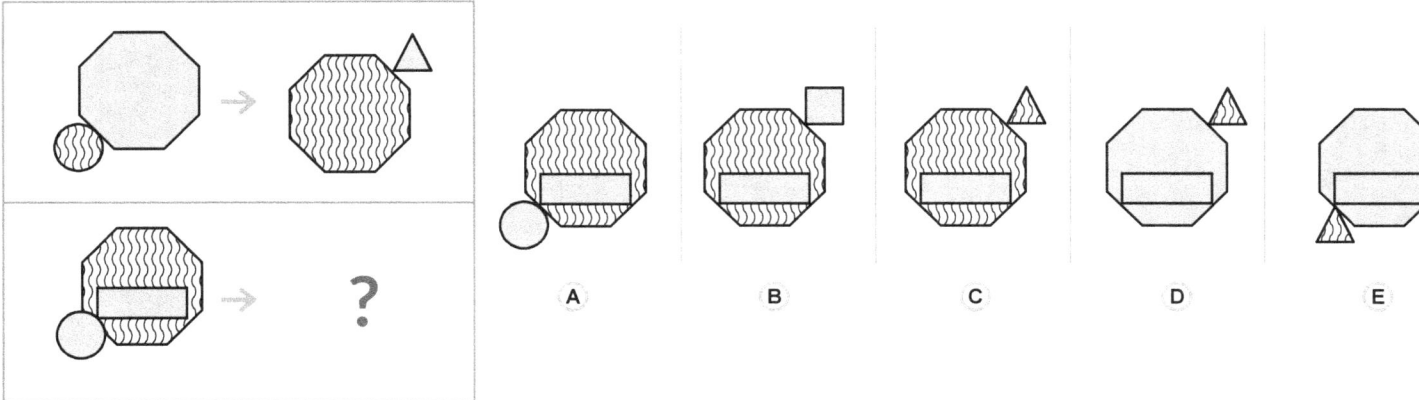

8

L =   I +
I L → L I

= =
L L → ?

+ +   = =   = =   + +   + +
= I   + +   L L   × =   I I
 A   B   C   D   E

9

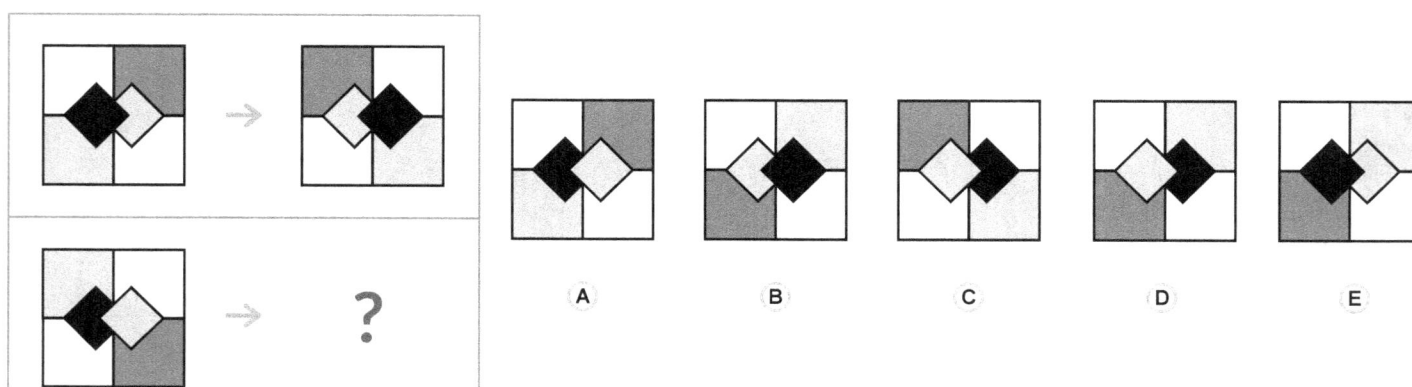

10

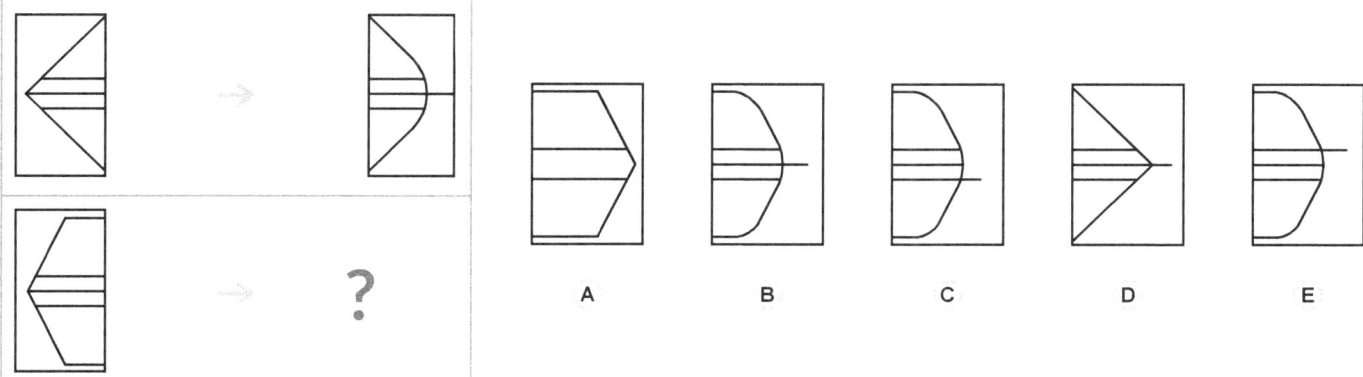

A   B   C   D   E

11

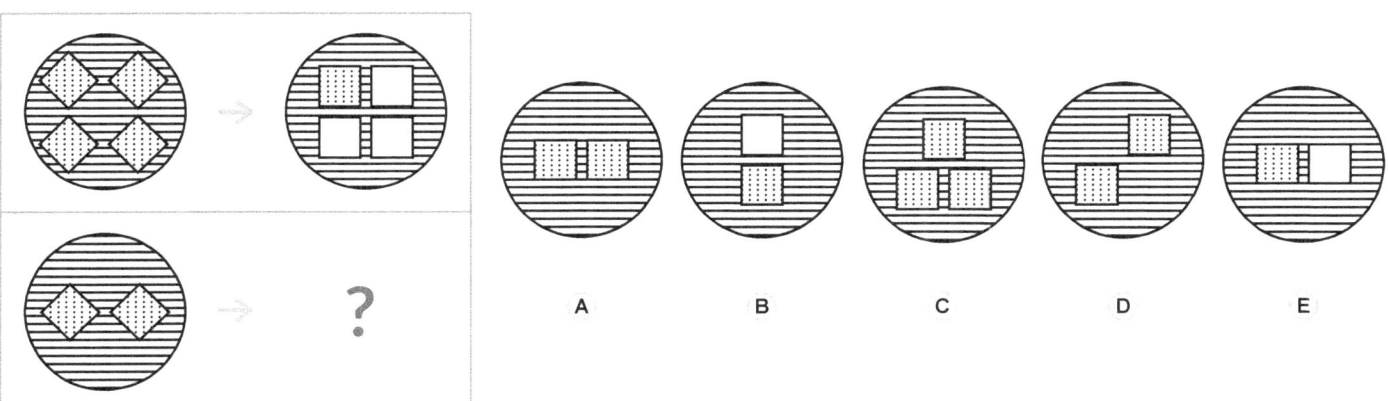

A   B   C   D   E

12

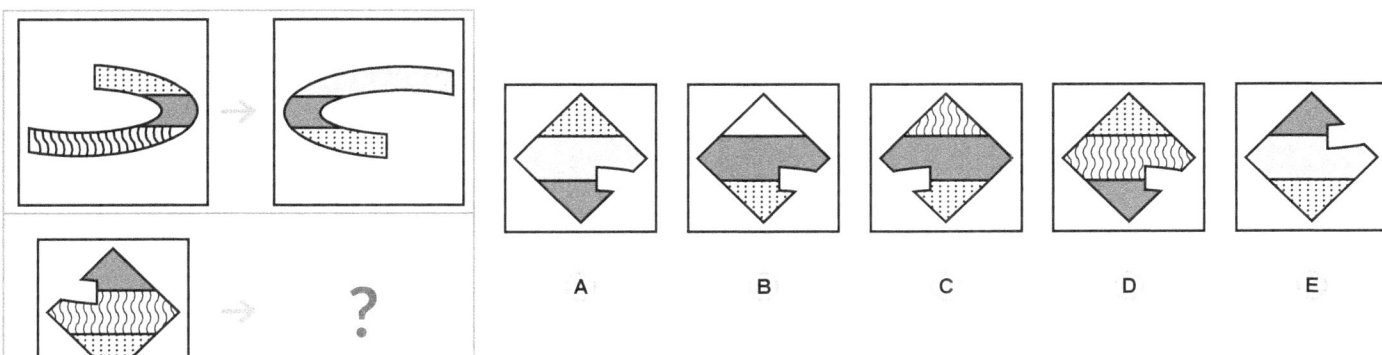

A   B   C   D   E

13

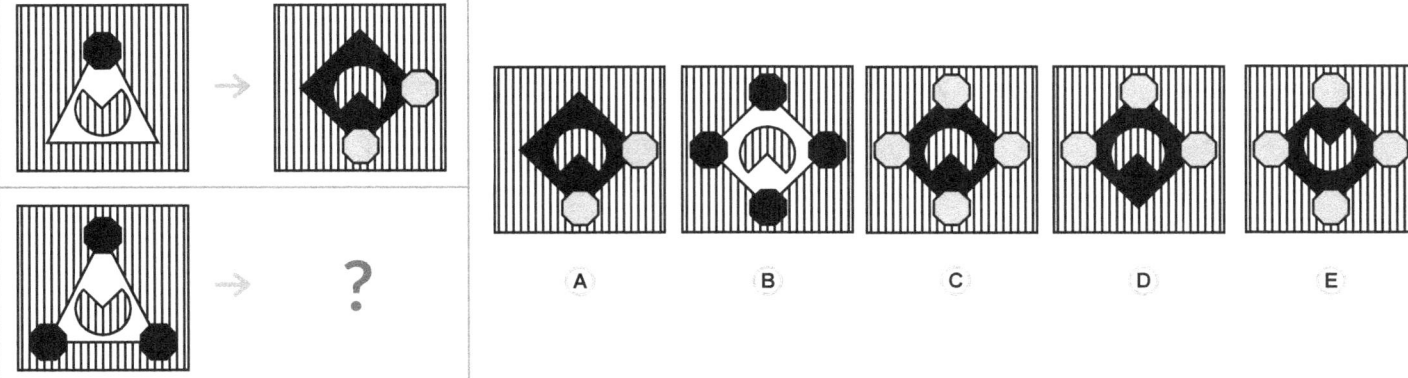

14

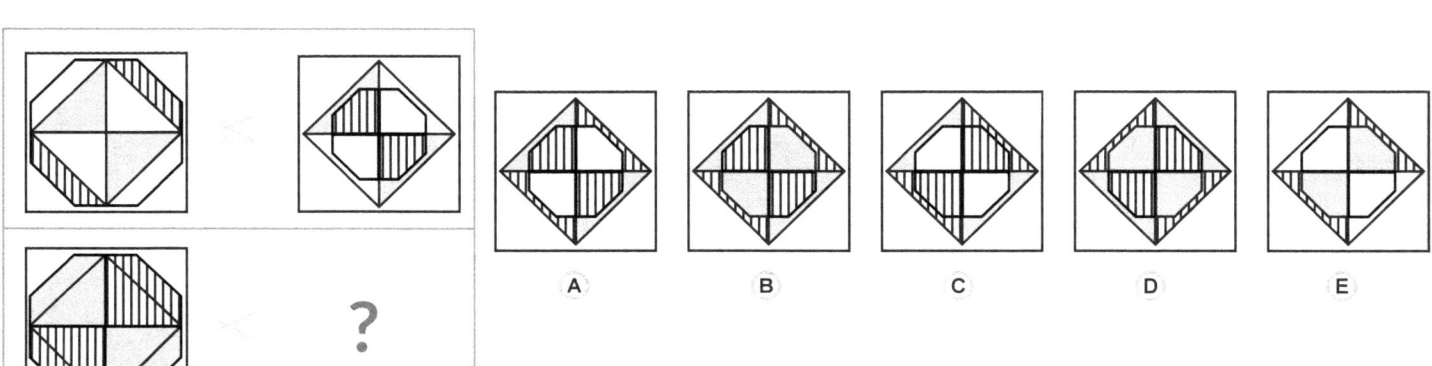

15

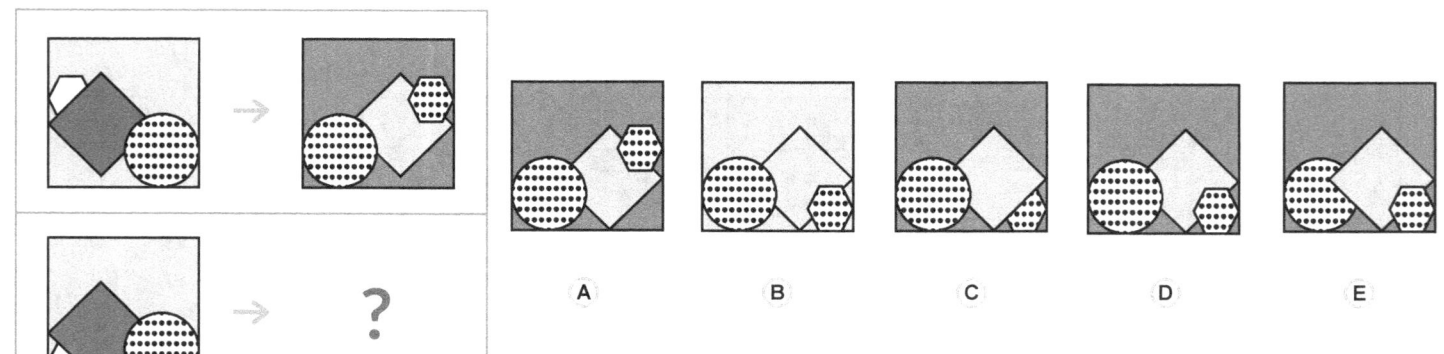

16

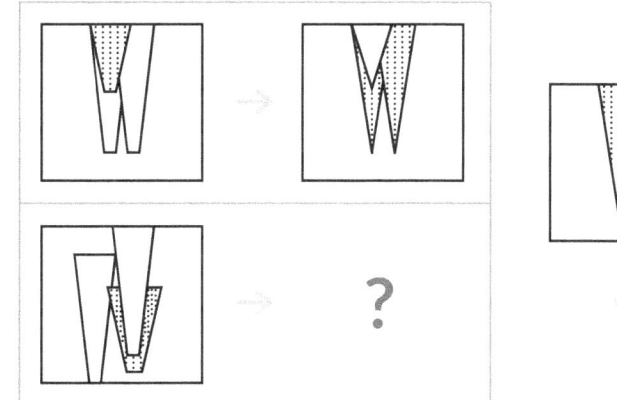

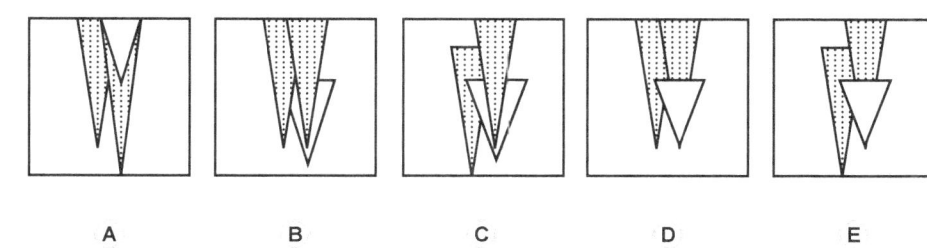

17

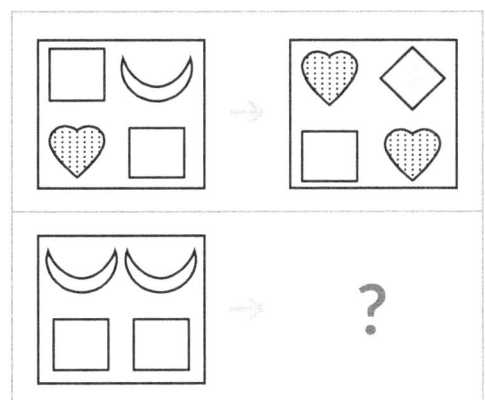

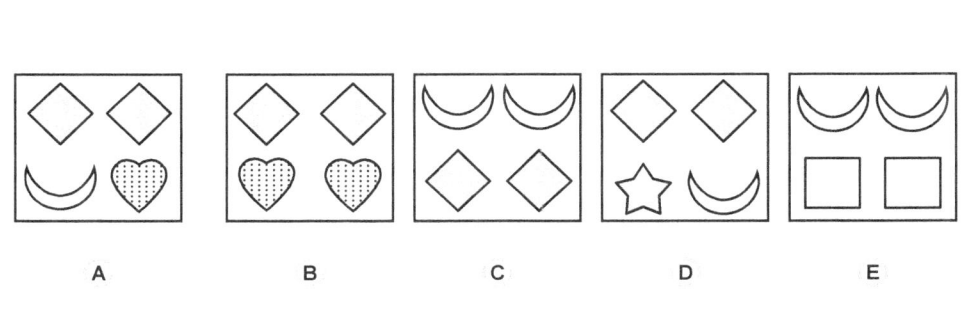

18

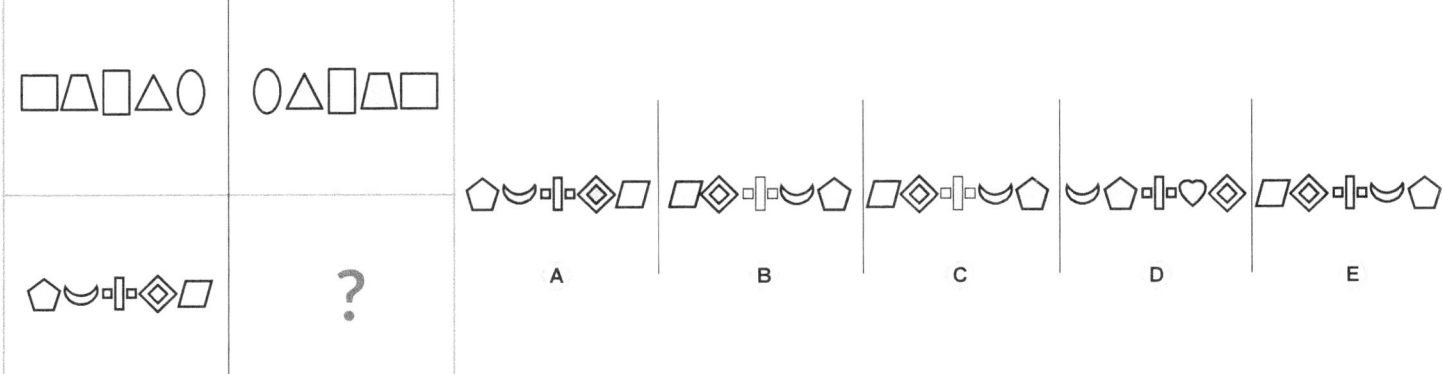

Paper Folding Directions: The top row shows a sheet of paper, how it was folded, and how holes were made in it. Which answer choice shows how the paper looks unfolded?

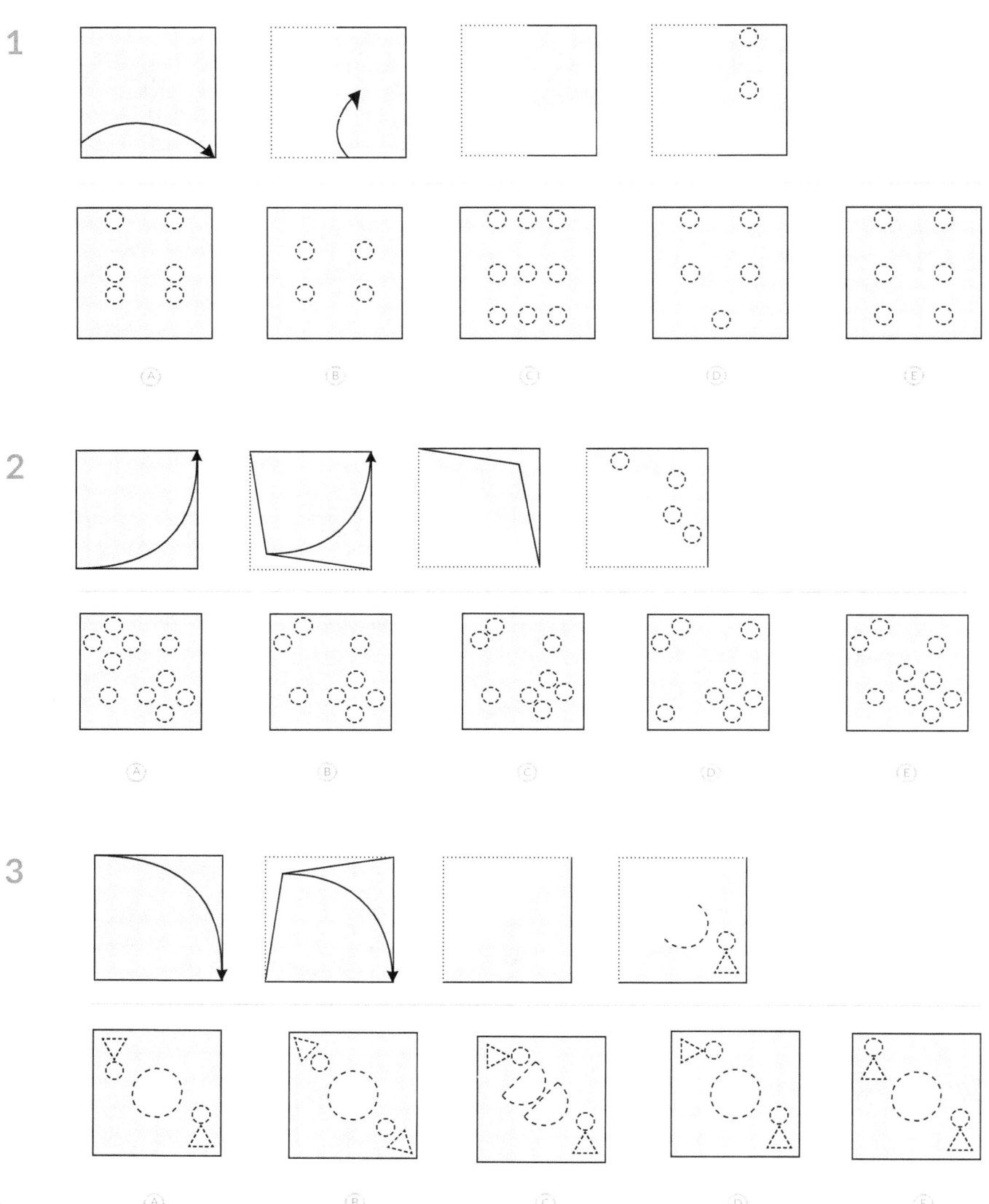

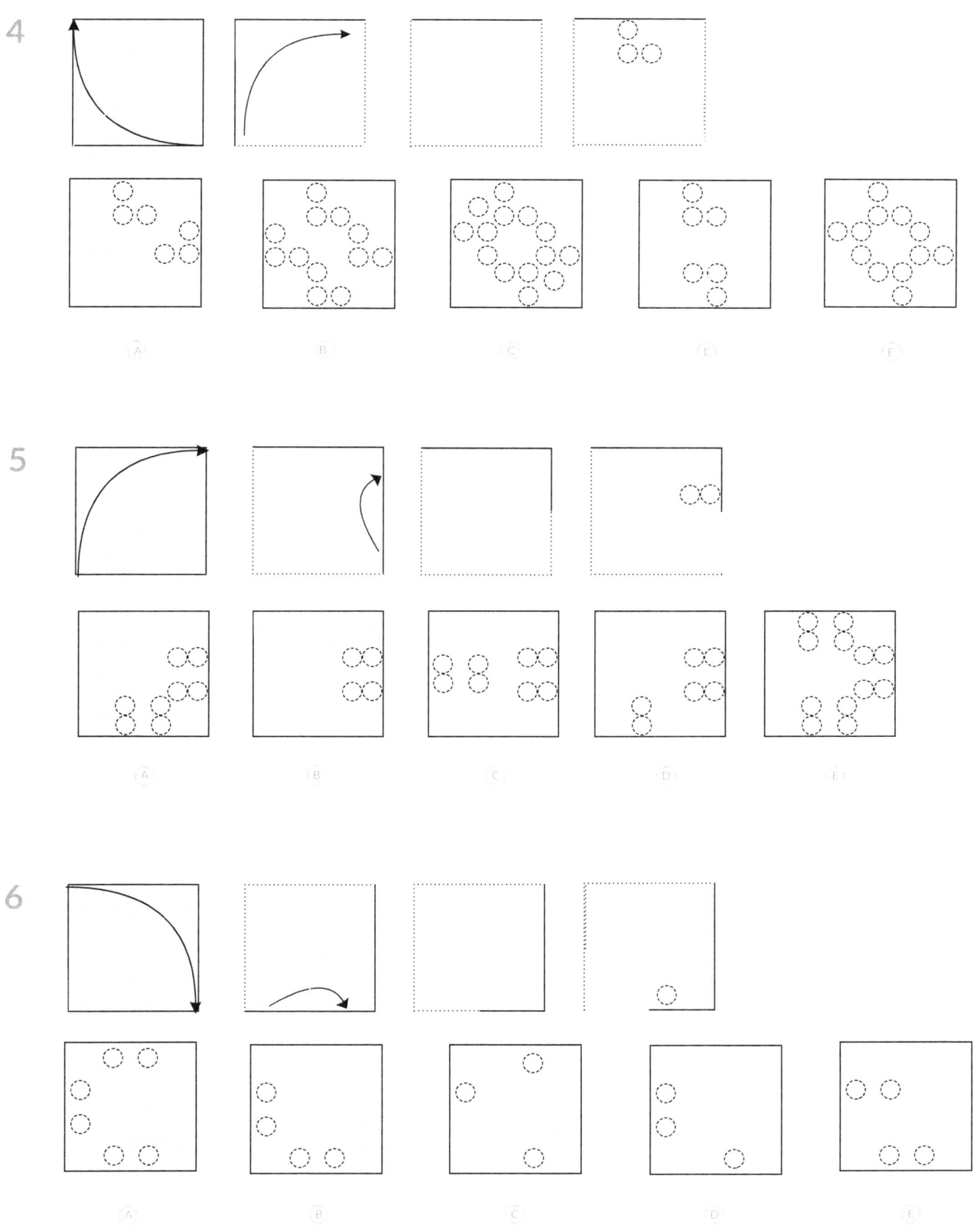

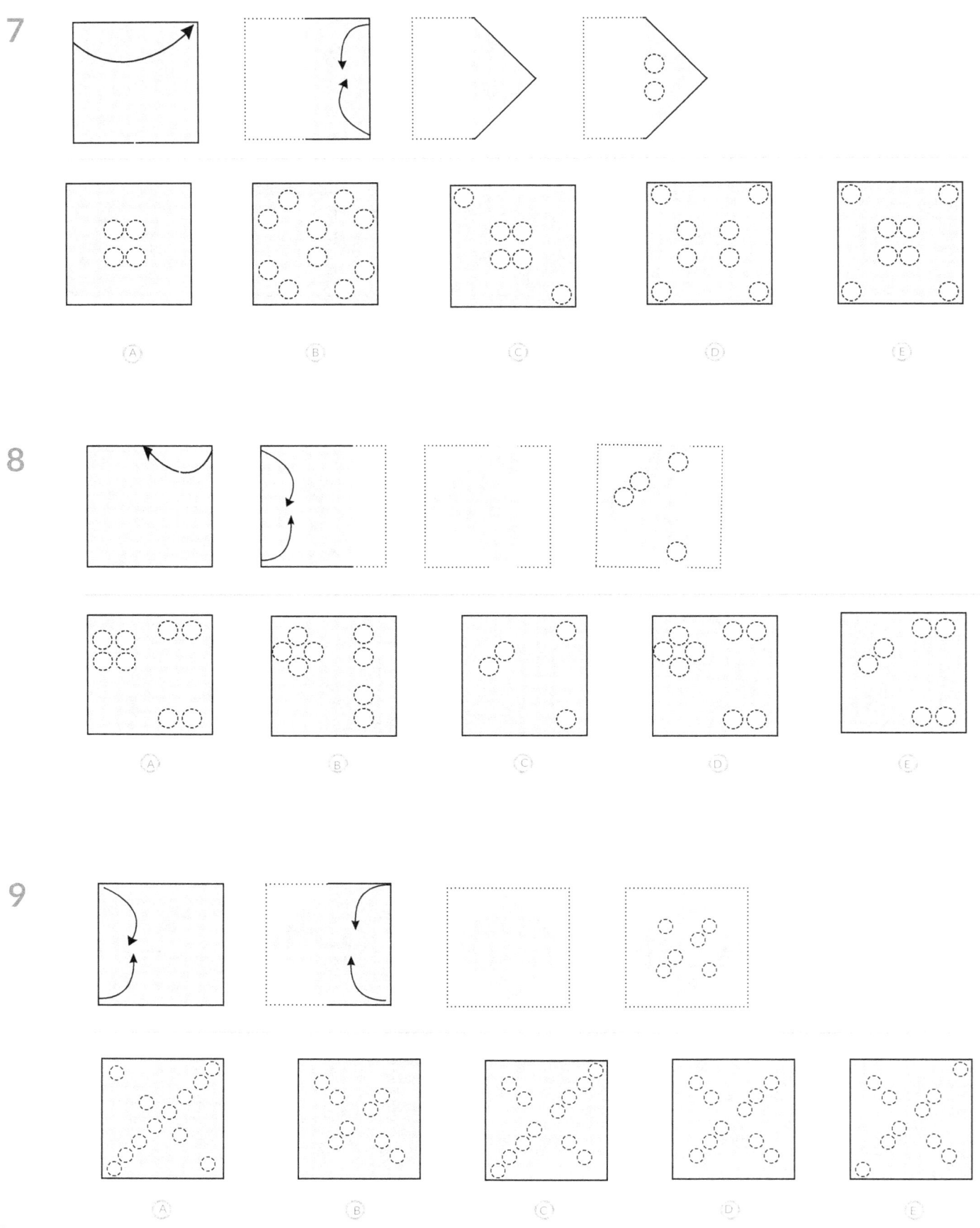

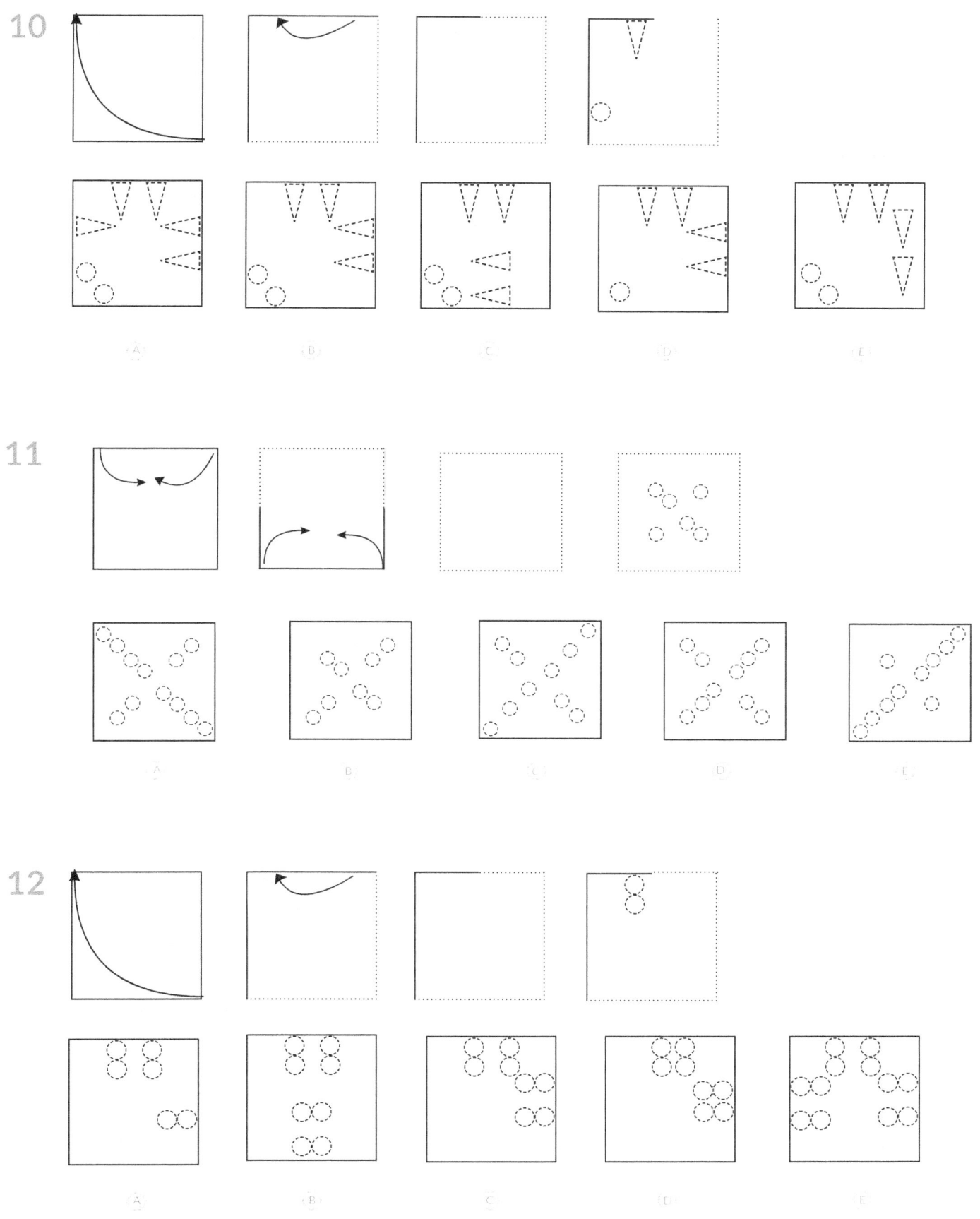

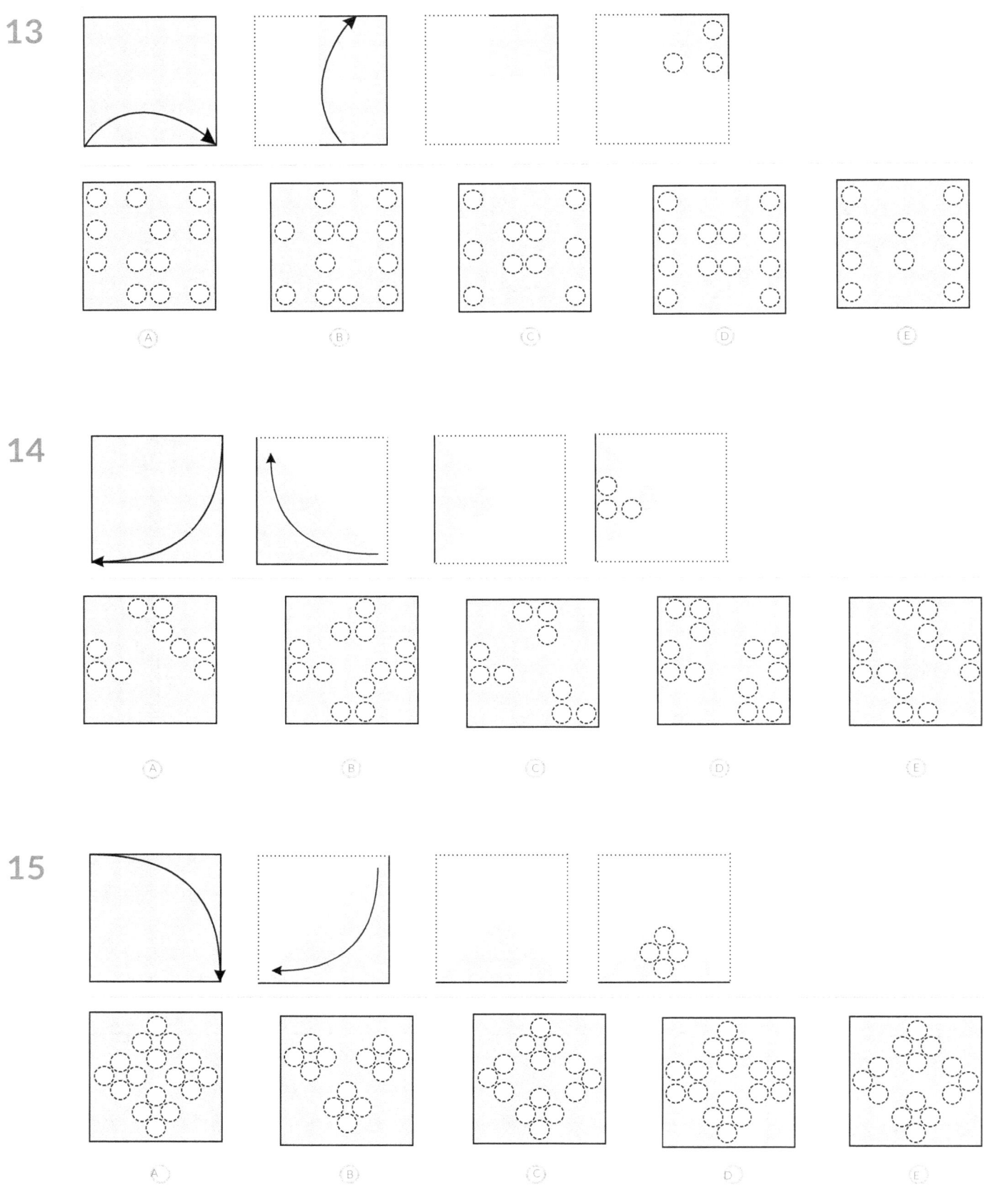

Number Puzzles Directions: What answer choice should you put in the place of the question mark so that both sides of the equal sign total the same amount?

1    $? \times 3.5 = 280$

   (A) 60   (B) 70   (C) 80   (D) 90   (E) 50

2    $864 = 12 \times ?$

   (A) 124   (B) 72   (C) 144   (D) 180   (E) 852

3    $25 + 0.5 = 20 + ?/10$

   (A) 30   (B) 20   (C) 25   (D) 15   (E) 55

4    $15 + 0.2 = 15 + ?/5$

   (A) 1   (B) 2   (C) 3   (D) 4   (E) 5

5    $? \times \blacksquare = 120$
     $\blacksquare = 15 - 5$

   (A) 8   (B) 9   (C) 12   (D) 15   (E) 10

6

$? \div \blacksquare = 7.2$

$\blacksquare = 5.5$

(A) 25.6   (B) 39.6   (C) 35.4   (D) 44.1   (E) 12.7

7

$? \times \blacksquare = 630$

$425 - \blacksquare = 320$

(A) 8   (B) 9   (C) 7   (D) 6   (E) 12

8

$\blacksquare - 17 = ? \times 5$

$\blacksquare = 94 \div 2$

(A) 4   (B) 5   (C) 6   (D) 7   (E) 15.8

9

$\blacksquare - 5.5 = ? \times 2$

$\blacksquare = 18 \div 1.5$

(A) 4   (B) 5   (C) 7   (D) 3.25   (E) 3.5

10

$? - \blacksquare = 150$

$320 - \blacksquare = 200 + 50$

(A) 466   (B) 420   (C) 350   (D) 220   (E) 370

11. ? - ■ = 125.5
    200.8 - ■ = 100.3 + 50.2

    Ⓐ 230.0   Ⓑ 275.5   Ⓒ 210.6   Ⓓ 250.7   Ⓔ 175.8

12. ■ ÷ 4 = ?
    ■ = 28 + ●
    ● = 50 - 32

    Ⓐ 15.5   Ⓑ 27.5   Ⓒ 19   Ⓓ 11.5   Ⓔ 17

13. ■ ÷ 3 = ?
    ■ = 45 + ●
    ● = 70 - 55

    Ⓐ 20   Ⓑ 56.7   Ⓒ 10   Ⓓ 30   Ⓔ 15

14. ■ ÷ 4 = ?
    ■ = 50 + ●
    ● = 62 - 31

    Ⓐ 18   Ⓑ 28   Ⓒ 31   Ⓓ 35.75   Ⓔ 20.25

15. ■ ÷ 4 = ?
    ■ = 19 + ●
    ● = 12 - 3

    Ⓐ 5   Ⓑ 7   Ⓒ 6   Ⓓ 4.5   Ⓔ 9

16 $\blacksquare \div 25 = ?$

$\blacksquare = 300 + \bullet$

$\bullet = 85 - 60$

(A) 8   (B) 10   (C) 12   (D) 13   (E) 25

17 $\blacksquare \div 5 = ?$

$\blacksquare = 15.8 + \bullet$

$\bullet = 8.4 - 3$

(A) 25.2   (B) 41   (C) 4.24   (D) 20.5   (E) 9.16

18 $\blacksquare \div 1/4 = ?$

$\blacksquare = 6 + \bullet$

$\bullet = 2/5 \times 15$

(A) 3   (B) 48   (C) 45   (D) 13   (E) 6

Number Analogies Directions: Look at the first two sets of numbers. Come up with a rule that both sets follow. Take this rule to figure out which answer choice goes in the place of the question mark.

1 **[112 → 8]**   **[126 → 9]**   **[154 → ?]**

    A 10   B 11   C 12   D 13   E 14

2 **[52.5 → 68.5]**   **[73.8 → 89.8]**   **[65.7 → ?]**

    A 83.7   B 80.7   C 82.7   D 84.7   E 81.7

3 **[0.20 → 1/5]**   **[0.75 → 3/4]**   **[0.40 → ?]**

    A 1/3   B 1/2   C 2/5   D 3/5   F 4/7

4 **[12 → 37]**   **[15 → 46]**   **[18 → ?]**

    A 49   B 53   C 56   D 55   E 57

5 **[54 → 28]**   **[82 → 42]**   **[76 → ?]**

    A 38   B 39   C 40   D 41   E 42

6   **[16 → 256]**   **[18 → 324]**   **[19 → ?]**

(A) 361   (B) 306   (C) 259   (D) 381   (E) 389

7   **[24 → 3]**   **[32 → 5]**   **[8 → ?]**

(A) -2   (B) -1   (C) 2   (D) -13   (E) 5

8   **[-2 → -11]**   **[-3 → -16]**   **[0 → ?]**

(A) -1   (B) 1   (C) 0   (D) 5   (E) -6

9   **[1.2 → 2.44]**   **[1.5 → 3.25]**   **[2.3 → ?]**

(A) 3.30   (B) 5.29   (C) 4.05   (D) 3.54   (E) 6.29

10   **[1 → 1]**   **[2 → 8]**   **[4 → ?]**

(A) 16   (B) 27   (C) 64   (D) 81   (E) 100

11   **[2 → 10]**   **[3 → 29]**   **[4 → ?]]**

    A. 66   B. 64   C. 62   D. 30   E. 12

12   **[1/2 → 1/4]**   **[3/5 → 9/25]**   **[2/3 → ?]**

    A. 2/9   B. 4/9   C. 3/8   D. 1/4   E. 1/3

13   **[6.4 → 4.2]**   **[9.6 → 5.8]**   **[12.8 → ?]**

    A. 6.4   B. 6.6   C. 7.2   D. 7.4   E. 7.6

14   **[1/4 → 1.0625]**   **[1/2 → 1.25]**   **[3/4 → ?]**

    A. 0.5625   B. 2.5   C. 1.5625   D. 1.75   E. 1.875

15   **[0.12 → 3/25]**   **[0.375 → 3/8]**   **[0.625 → ?]**

    A. 5/8   B. 5/6   C. 4/7   D. 9/16   E. 7/9

16   **[5.2 → 2.3]**   **[7.6 → 2.9]**   **[10.8 → ?]**

(A) 2.7   (B) 1.7   (C) 6.1   (D) 7.9   (E) 3.7

17   **[1/2 → 1/8]**   **[2/3 → 8/27]**   **[3/4 → ?]**

(A) 9/16   (B) 27/64   (C) 27/32   (D) 8/27   (E) 81/256

18   **[3.2 → 5.8]**   **[8.4 → 7.1]**   **[10.8 → ?]**

(A) 2.7   (B) -2.3   (C) 7.7   (D) 7.8   (E) 1.8

19   **[1/2 → 5½]**   **[1/4 → 2¾]**   **[3/5 → ?]**

(A) 6⅗   (B) 6⅕   (C) 7⅕   (D) 8⅕   (E) 5⅖

20   **[0.5 → 0.125]**   **[1.2 → 1.728]**   **[1.5 → ?]**

(A) 1.625   (B) 3.375   (C) 2.375   (D) 2.972   (E) 2.25

Number Series Directions: Which answer choice would complete the pattern?

1   **12.7**   **51.7**   **90.7**   **129.7**   **?**

- A) 139.7
- B) 170.7
- C) 178.7
- D) 168.7
- E) 168.0

2   **2.5**   **10**   **40**   **160**   **?**

- A) 64.0
- B) 320
- C) 620
- D) 640
- E) 700

3   **40**   **3**   **40**   **6**   **40**   **12**   **40**   **?**

- A) 18
- B) 40
- C) 24
- D) 16
- E) 20

4   **22**   **78.8**   **22**   **39.4**   **22**   **?**

- A) 11.7
- B) 19.7
- C) 22
- D) 19.2
- E) 22.1

5   **10.5**   **9.5**   **7.5**   **6.5**   **4.5**   **?**

- A) 2.5
- B) 1.5
- C) 3.5
- D) 0.5
- E) 5.5

6   15   46   78   111   145   ?

(A) 182   (B) 181   (C) 183   (D) 184   (E) 180

7   20   19   18   16   15   14   ?

(A) 13   (B) 12   (C) 11   (D) 10   (E) 9

8   6.5   5.5   11   10   20   ?

(A) 40   (B) 39   (C) 21   (D) 41   (E) 19

9   1/16   1/4   1/8   1/2   1/4   ?

(A) 2   (B) 1/2   (C) 1/16   (D) 1   (E) 1/4

10   15.5   3.5   13.5   5.5   11.5   7.5   9.5   9.5   ?

(A) 11.5   (B) 8.5   (C) 7.5   (D) 9.5   (E) 6.5

11   **20**   **17**   **14**   **15**   **12**   9   **10**   7   **4**   **5**   **?**

(A) 2   (B) 1   (C) 0   (D) 3   (E) -1

12   **4**   **4**   **4**   **4**   **8**   **16**   **8**   **24**   **72**   **?**

(A) 18   (B) 24   (C) 36   (D) 48   (E) 54

13   **12.5**   **9.5**   **5.5**   **0.5**   **-5.5**   **-12.5**   **-20.5**   **?**

(A) 29.5   (B) 30.5   (C) -29.5   (D) -31.5   (E) -30.5

14   **10.5**   **-9.5**   **8.5**   **-7.5**   **6.5**   **-5.5**   **4.5**   **?**

(A) -3.5   (B) 3.5   (C) -4.5   (D) 2.5   (E) -2.5

15   **5.5**   **-0.5**   **3.5**   **-1.5**   **1.5**   **-2.5**   **-0.5**   **?**

(A) -1.5   (B) 0.5   (C) -3.5   (D) 1.5   (E) -2.5

16   -3   -7   -9   2   -27   11 ?

  Ⓐ -16   Ⓑ -81   Ⓒ -54   Ⓓ 20   Ⓔ 34

17   1/8   1/4   3/4   1.5   4.5   ?

  Ⓐ 8   Ⓑ 7   Ⓒ 12   Ⓓ 9   Ⓔ 6

18   50   47   51   46   40   47   39   30   40   ?

  Ⓐ 31   Ⓑ 18   Ⓒ 29   Ⓓ 25   Ⓔ 28

19   300   270   310   260   200   270   190   100   200 ?

  Ⓐ 90   Ⓑ 180   Ⓒ 100   Ⓓ 110   Ⓔ -10

20   -2.5   -3.5   -1.5   -4.5   -8.5   -3.5   -9.5   -16.5   -8.5 ?

  Ⓐ -9.5   Ⓑ -18.5   Ⓒ -19.5   Ⓓ -16.5   Ⓔ -17.5

PRACTICE TEST 1 ANSWER KEY

Verbal Classification, Practice Test 1

_____ 1. E. birds of prey _____ 2. C. types of scientists _____ 3. C. having to do with 3
_____ 4. A. different parts of a book's content (others are related to books but are not specific parts of a book's content)
_____ 5. A. adjectives describing something very strong/powerful
_____ 6. D. related to copying or reproducing something
_____ 7. B. modes of transport that do not carry many passengers (a few or just one)
_____ 8. A. modes of transport primarily used for leisure (not work) _____ 9. A. having to do with ending or stopping
_____ 10. D. related to continuing or keeping something going
_____ 11. B. relate to making something happen more quickly or increasing its speed
_____ 12. E. scientists who study different aspects of the Earth and its natural phenomena
_____ 13. A. words that describe height _____ 14. B. adjectives that describe emotions/feelings
_____ 15. C. scientists who study objects/people from the past
_____ 16. C. related to coming together or combining elements for a common purpose or goal
_____ 17. D. the top/highest point _____ 18. A. different forms of government
_____ 19. B. adjectives meaning very similar or identical _____ 20. E. adjectives describing large quantity/variety

Verbal Analogies, Practice Test 1

_____ 1. C. alphabetical order = organized by letter; chronological = organized by time
_____ 2. C. object > purpose _____ 3. D. opposites
_____ 4. A. A lantern was used in the past for lighting as a flashlight is today. A telegraph was used in the past for communication as a telephone is today.
_____ 5. E. large form > very small form _____ 6. E. opposites
_____ 7. A. Brilliant means very smart. Deafening means very loud.
_____ 8. C. Something dense has a lot of mass. Something bright has a lot of light.
_____ 9. D. object > place where objects are stored, preserved, and sometimes displayed
_____ 10. D. mild form > very strong form (of wind; of rain) _____ 11. B. object > object's top
_____ 12. B. Carelessness harms safety as corruption harms integrity.
_____ 13. C. Curiosity leads to discovery as innovation leads to advancement.
_____ 14. E. synonyms _____ 15. A. Something very frugal is economical. Something very transparent is clear.
_____ 16. B. opposites _____ 17. C. Negligence may cause an accident as a disease may cause an epidemic.
_____ 18. D. Preparation leads to readiness, just as training leads to proficiency.
_____ 19. C. Something very hostile is belligerent. Something very calm is placid.
_____ 20. E. Something elusive is difficult to capture, just as an enigma is difficult to solve.

Sentence Completion, Practice Test 1

_____ 1. D. elated = feeling extremely happy or excited
_____ 2. C. significantly = to a notable or important degree
_____ 3. E. barren = lacking vegetation or life
_____ 4. D. delicate = easily broken or damaged
_____ 5. B. rare = unique or uncommon
_____ 6. A. bias = an inclination or tendency to favor one thing over another
_____ 7. D. bolster = to support or strengthen
_____ 8. E. depleted = depleted soil has lost its essential nutrients and minerals
_____ 9. C. distinctive = having a quality or characteristic that makes something easily recognizable/ different
_____ 10. B. trepidation = a feeling of fear or anxiety about something that might happen
_____ 11. A. dismayed = feeling distress or disappointment
_____ 12. E. critique = an analysis/evaluation; significance = the importance or meaning
_____ 13. D. escalate = to increase in intensity, severity, or magnitude, often rapidly
_____ 14. A. formidable = inspiring fear or respect due to being large, powerful
_____ 15. B. groundbreaking = innovative and significant; intensified = increased in strength or degree
_____ 16. A. emphasize = to give special importance or prominence to something; vibrant = full of energy and bright, making it stand out
_____ 17. E. intriguing = arousing curiosity or interest; multifaceted = having many aspects or features
_____ 18. D. realize = to bring to completion; critical = absolutely necessary or essential
_____ 19. C. assemble = to gather; opportunity = a favorable moment or chance for something important
_____ 20. D. prevalent = widespread or commonly occurring; exist = to be present or have reality

Figure Classification, Practice Test 1

_____ 1. D. a star & triangle are inside the square's sections & they are opposite each other
_____ 2. E. trapezoids pointing left   _____ 3. D. shapes alternate: gray and wavy lines
_____ 4. E. 9-sided shapes
_____ 5. A. 1 of each shape: upside down pac-man, octagon, circle -and- 1 is either gray, white, or black
_____ 6. B. inside shape is 1 circle of each color: black, dark gray, light gray
_____ 7. E. half of shape is gray/half is filled with dots   _____ 8. C. right shape has 1 more side than left shape
_____ 9. A. the bottom shape is the same as the top shape but has been rotated 90° clockwise (to the right); the inside pattern also changes from dotted to white
_____ 10. E. as figures rotate, circle remains at same point on "L" shape -OR- figures rotate 90° clockwise
_____ 11. D. small center shape & outer shape have same design/color inside -and- the shapes are different kinds of shapes
_____ 12. B. in the group of 2 shapes, the larger shape has 1 more side than the smaller shape
_____ 13. A. 1 shape points up, 3 shapes point down
_____ 14. C. diagonal line goes from lower left to upper right inside shape
_____ 15. E. tic-tac-toe with rectangles
_____ 16. B. inside square are 3 shapes: square that's next to an oval and a trapezoid that is not
_____ 17. D. one-quarter of shape has been "cut"
_____ 18. A. the square is divided into 3 triangles; in the largest is a smaller triangle; in the smaller 2 & on opposite sides as the smaller triangle is a small half-triangle & square
_____ 19. E. order of shapes from bottom to top: square - crescent - oval

Questions Answered Correctly: _____ out of 19

Figure Analogies, Practice Test 1

_____ 1. C.
_____ 2. E. inside the square, the shape's number of sides increases by 1
_____ 3. D. colors switch in the divided circle; colors switch in the divided triangle
_____ 4. C. the shapes "flip in" & move 90° clockwise
_____ 5. E. shapes "flip" to become a mirror image
_____ 6. A. shape group "flips" & the dotted rectangle covers left half of center shape
_____ 7. E. shape group rotates 90° counterclockwise & the outer 2 smaller shapes change color
_____ 8. C. group of triangles "flips"/is a mirror image (note that in the bottom box, when you flip the 2 shapes on the right, choice C is the only choice with the dark gray arrow & white shapes flipped correctly)
_____ 9. E. dark gray becomes light gray; dotted becomes dark gray; light gray becomes dotted -or- the last shape becomes the first shape
_____ 10. B. since the figures are the same, they change the same way
_____ 11. A. from left to right, larger shape will have 2 less sides, smaller shape will have +1 side; colors of large & small shapes reverse
_____ 12. C. shapes change like this: left pointing arch becomes a square; down pointing arch becomes a triangle pointing up; up pointing arch becomes a heart
_____ 13. B. top shape goes inside bottom shape & gets bigger; middle shape goes inside & rotates 90° clockwise
_____ 14. D. upper left figure rotates 180° to face down; upper right & lower right shapes switch and the new upper right becomes gray
_____ 15. C. shapes change to hexagons; note that the shapes are divided into quarters & the dark quarters change positions like this (bottom left > bottom right; top left > bottom left; bottom right > top left; top right stays the same)
_____ 16. E. top shape rotates 180°; shape on left moves right; bottom shape flips & changes from light gray to dark gray
_____ 17. D. the bottom moves to the top; the top moves to the middle; the middle goes to the bottom; then the shapes are placed over each other rather than under
_____ 18. A. shape group rotates 180°
_____ 19. C. top shape goes inside middle shape; top shape & middle shape get bigger; bottom shape becomes the center shape, rotates 90° counterclockwise, and becomes gray

Questions Answered Correctly: _____ out of 19

Paper Folding, Practice Test 1

_____ 1. D   _____ 2. E   _____ 3. C   _____ 4. D   _____ 5. B   _____ 6. C   _____ 7. A
_____ 8. C   _____ 9. A   _____ 10. E   _____ 11. B   _____ 12. A   _____ 13. E   _____ 14. C
_____ 15. E   _____ 16. C   _____ 17. B

Questions Answered Correctly: _____ out of 17

Number Puzzles, Practice Test 1

_____ 1. B   _____ 2. C   _____ 3. C   _____ 4. E   _____ 5. A   _____ 6. E   _____ 7. D
_____ 8. D   _____ 9. B   _____ 10. A   _____ 11. B   _____ 12. C   _____ 13. E   _____ 14. D
_____ 15. B   _____ 16. C   _____ 17. E   _____ 18. A

Questions Answered Correctly: _____ out of 18

Number Analogies, Practice Test 1

_____ 1. B. x12 _____ 2. C. divide 15 _____ 3. E. squared _____ 4. A. divide by 10
_____ 5. D. decimal is converted to its equivalent fraction form _____ 6. C. x2, then +1
_____ 7. B. x3, then -1 _____ 8. C. square number, then +1 _____ 9. D. ÷ by 2, then +1
_____ 10. E. divide by 4, then +3 _____ 11. A. x3, then +4 _____ 12. D. raise to 3rd power
_____ 13. A. raise to third power, then -1 _____ 14. B. x4, then +1 _____ 15. A. squared, then -3
_____ 16. E. divide by 4, then +1 _____ 17. D. squared _____ 18. C. divide by 4, +1

Questions Answered Correctly: _____ out of 18

Number Series, Practice Test 1

_____ 1. D. x3 _____ 2. E. -29
_____ 3. B. every other number is 29; starting from 60, every other number increases by 5
_____ 4. E. -1, -2, -1, -2, etc. _____ 5. A. +1, +2, +1, +2 _____ 6. C. -21, -22, -23, -24, -25, etc.
_____ 7. B. +1, +1, +2; +1, +1, +2, etc.
_____ 8. D. each number in the series is multiplied by an increasing factor: 5 x 2 = 10, 10 x 3 = 30, 30 x 4 = 120, etc.
_____ 9. D. every other number is 44; starting from 56, every other number is divided by 2
_____ 10. A. +1, +1, +2; +1, +1, +2, etc. _____ 11. C. ×2, +1, ×2, +1, etc. _____ 12. E. ×4, ÷2, ×4, ÷2
_____ 13. B. +8, −3, +7, +8, −3, +7
_____ 14. C. numbers in positions 1, 3, 5, 7, 9 (odd positions) increase by 1; numbers in positions 2, 4, 6, 8 (even positions) also increase by 1 -OR- the difference between each pair of numbers (1st & 2nd, 3rd & 4th, etc.) is always 15
_____ 15. A. numbers in positions 1, 3, 5, 7, 9 (odd positions) decrease by 2; numbers in positions 2, 4, 6, 8 (even positions) increase by 2
_____ 16. E. +2, +2, −1, +2, +2, −1, etc. _____ 17. D. +1, +1,−1; +2, +2, −2; +3, +3, −3
_____ 18. B. ×2, ×2, ÷2; ×2, ×2, ÷2, etc. _____ 19. B. numbers increase like this: +3, +4, +5, +6, +7, +8, +9, etc.
_____ 20. C. -6, +5, -4, +3, -2, +1, etc.

Questions Answered Correctly: _____ out of 20

PRACTICE TEST 2 ANSWER KEY

Verbal Classification, Practice Test 2

_____ 1. C. wild cats _____ 2. A. vehicles whose main function is transporting people (not cargo/materials)
_____ 3. B. scientists who study living things _____ 4. D. related to improvement/making something better
_____ 5. E. the lowest part/deepest point of something _____ 6. A. things that provide cover
_____ 7. D. skills that require training/must be learned _____ 8. E. places used for storage
_____ 9. C. verbs describing different movement types _____ 10. C. related to breaking apart or separating into parts
_____ 11. A. adjectives describing a limited or small amount _____ 12. B. things used for display purposes
_____ 13. D. verbs describing actions of standing still or staying in one place _____ 14. E. bodies of water
_____ 15. B. printed material
_____ 16. C. verbs related to calculating or determining something based on available data
_____ 17. D. types of awards or forms of recognition given for achievements _____ 18. B. living things
_____ 19. A. verbs involved with moving/traveling from one place to another

Questions Answered Correctly: _____ out of 19

Verbal Analogies, Practice Test 2

_____ 1. E. A fragment is a broken piece of metal, just as a crumb is a broken piece of bread.
_____ 2. D. An artist is a type of occupation. A cathedral is a type of monument.
_____ 3. B. Accumulate is a synonym of gather, just as disperse is a synonym of scatter.
_____ 4. A. A glimmer is a mild form of light. A blaze is a strong form. A murmur is a mild form of sound. A shout is a strong form.
_____ 5. C. An encyclopedia was used in the past for information retrieval as the internet is used today. A map was used in the past in the same way a GPS is used today.
_____ 6. E. Malnutrition harms health, just as misinformation harms accuracy.
_____ 7. C. Study leads to comprehension, just as practice leads to expertise.
_____ 8. B. When length decreases, it is shortened. When complexity decreases, it is simplified.
_____ 9. A. When someone is apathetic, they are without emotion. When something is silent, it is without noise.
_____ 10. E. Something elaborate is very complex. Something momentous is very significant.
_____ 11. D. An atom is a small part of a larger molecule, just as a verse is a small part of a larger poem.
_____ 12. B. An editor's role is to revise, just as a translator's role is to interpret.
_____ 13. A. If there is harmony, there is no discord. If there is clarity, there is no confusion.
_____ 14. D. A chisel is a tool used in sculpture. A scalpel is a tool used in surgery.
_____ 15. C. Something profound is very deep. Something arduous is very challenging.
_____ 16. E. Antonyms
_____ 17. A. An innovative person has a lot of creativity, just as a resolute person has a lot of determination.
_____ 18. D. Synonyms _____ 19. C. If something is infallible, it has no error. If something is immutable, it has no change.
_____ 20. B. Synonyms

Questions Answered Correctly: _____ out of 20

Sentence Completion, Practice Test 2

_____ 1. C. precise = exact and accurate in measurement or description
_____ 2. B. enthusiastic = showing intense and eager interest or excitement about something
_____ 3. E. pristine = something that is in its original, pure, or unspoiled condition
_____ 4. B. fondness = a liking or affection for something
_____ 5. E. malfunction = failure to function normally or properly
_____ 6. C. facilitate = to make an action or process easier
_____ 7. A. contaminated = made impure or unsafe by exposure to harmful substances or pollutants
_____ 8. D. original = something that is new, unique
_____ 9. C. dramatically = something happening in a big or noticeable way
_____ 10. A. exasperated = feeling frustrated or annoyed
_____ 11. A. remarkable = worthy of attention due to being unusual or impressive; heightened = increased or intensified
_____ 12. B. underscore = to emphasize or highlight something; bold = a style that is prominent and stands out
_____ 13. E. captivating = highly interesting or engaging; engaging = attracting or holding attention
_____ 14. D. attain = achieve; imperative = absolutely necessary/required
_____ 15. C. converge = to come together; occasion = a special time or event that provides an opportunity
_____ 16. A. divergent = differing; varied = showing differences
_____ 17. B. amplify = to increase strength of something; appeal = attractiveness/interest
_____ 18. E. control = to manage or regulate; essential = absolutely necessary
_____ 19. D. strenuous = demanding, requiring a lot of effort; altitudes = heights above sea level
_____ 20. B. minimize = to reduce the risk or impact; implements = to put into effect

Questions Answered Correctly: _____ out of 20

Figure Classification, Practice Test 2

_____ 1. E. 4-sided shape with a smaller 4-sided shape inside
_____ 2. A. inside circle is a: division sign, oval, diamond, pac-man
_____ 3. D. inside larger shape are 2 small horizontally-aligned circles with same color
_____ 4. D. in triangle are 3 shapes, 2 are the same kind of shape & same size; 1 is gray & 1 has lines; a 3rd shape has lines
_____ 5. E. shape is divided into equal parts
_____ 6. E. shape with wavy lines has 1 more side than shape with diagonal lines
_____ 7. B. rectangle has straight lines that are aligned vertically
_____ 8. A. each group has an octagon, parallelogram, hexagon; they are either white or filled with diagonal lines
_____ 9. B. as trapezoid rotates, its sections remain in the same order and the trapezoid must be the same size (E is smaller)
_____ 10. E. 1 darker gray & 1 lighter gray opposite each other; 4 sections of inner square have different designs
_____ 11. C. smaller inner shapes are 3 diamonds & 6 squares
_____ 12. B. larger shape has diagonal wavy lines going from lower left to upper right
_____ 13. A. 1 corner (and only 1 corner) has the same group of 3 shapes: trapezoid on top, circle & square on bottom
_____ 14. C. when you put the shape group on its base (the double lines), the order is the same
_____ 15. D. squares have formed "tic-tac-toe", plus a single rectangle is in a corner
_____ 16. E. crescents & diamonds are in opposite sections of the divided larger shape (crescents & diamonds must be opposite each other)
_____ 17. B. larger shapes & smaller trapezoids have different designs (dots vs. lines) -and- the trapezoids point to one of the larger shape's corners
_____ 18. E. bottom shape is same as top shape, but the top shape has been rotated 90° clockwise (to the right) and it changes colors

Questions Answered Correctly: _____ out of 18

Figure Analogies, Practice Test 2

_____ 1. C. light gray shape 'flips' down, dark gray shape added on top that's facing the original position of the first shape
_____ 2. E. in the sections of the squares/parallelograms, the colors/designs change like this: dotted becomes black, black becomes gray, and gray becomes dotted; also, the original outer shape does not change
_____ 3. D. bottom shape becomes top shape & gets smaller, middle shape becomes bottom shape & gets bigger, top shape becomes middle shape & gets bigger
_____ 4. E. group of figures shows 3 "half" shapes; from left to right, largest half has 5 sides, then 3 sides; middle half points down, then up; smallest half has rounded corners, then a version of this same half, but with straight corners
_____ 5. A. on top, dark gray rectangle with 1/4 filled w/ diagonal lines becomes a circle filled with dots and the same amount (1/4) filled with diagonal lines; on the bottom, the dotted rectangle with 1/2 filled w/ diagonal lines becomes dark gray circle with same amount (1/2) filled with dark gray; note that the design & quantity of the inside lines must be the same also
_____ 6. B. the shape group rotates 90° clockwise, then the gray circles become filled with dots and vice versa
_____ 7. D. in top set, octagon switches from gray to wavy lines; lower left circle changes to a triangle, moves to the upper right, and the design inside changes from wavy lines to gray; in the bottom, the reverse occurs: octagon changes from filled with wavy lines to gray, circle changes to a triangle & changes its position and design (gray to wavy); no change with rectangle
_____ 8. E. "L" becomes "I"; equal sign becomes plus; "I" becomes "L"; equal sign becomes plus sign
_____ 9. D. mirror image of original figure
_____ 10. B. corners of shape become rounded & middle line gets longer
_____ 11. E. small shapes change from diamonds to squares and are horizontally aligned & all except 1 changes from dotted to white

CONTINUED ON THE NEXT PAGE

Figure Analogies, Practice Test 2, Continued

_____ 12. A. shape rotates 180° & wavy lines become light gray

_____ 13. C. white triangles become black diamonds; center shape (the pac-man) rotates 180°; one more octagon is added -and- all the octagons change from black to gray

_____ 14. B. inside & outside shape switch positions & get smaller; with the new inner shape (the octagon), the lined pattern & the solid color have switched; with the new outer shape (the diamond), the gray & the other section remain the same

_____ 15. D. shape group becomes a "mirror image", then the hexagon moves in front of the diamond and becomes filled with dots; diamond changes from dark gray to light gray; large square changes from light gray to dark gray

_____ 16. C. shapes in first box (thin trapezoids) change to triangles & the colors/patterns of the shapes reverse

_____ 17. B. white squares become hearts filled with dots; white crescents become gray diamonds; hearts filled with dots become white squares

_____ 18. E. order of shapes reverses -and- the 2nd shape & the 4th shape turn gray

Questions Answered Correctly: _____ out of 18

Paper Folding, Practice Test 2

_____ 1. E _____ 2. B _____ 3. D _____ 4. E _____ 5. A _____ 6. B _____ 7. E
_____ 8. D _____ 9. C _____ 10. B _____ 11. A _____ 12. C _____ 13. D _____ 14. E
_____ 15. A

Questions Answered Correctly: _____ out of 15

Number Puzzles, Practice Test 2

_____ 1. C _____ 2. B _____ 3. E _____ 4. A _____ 5. C _____ 6. B _____ 7. D
_____ 8. C _____ 9. D _____ 10. D _____ 11. E _____ 12. D _____ 13. A _____ 14. E
_____ 15. B _____ 16. D _____ 17. C _____ 18. B

Questions Answered Correctly: _____ out of 18

Number Analogies, Practice Test 2

_____ 1. B. divide by 14 _____ 2. E. +16 _____ 3. C. decimal is converted to its equivalent fraction form
_____ 4. D. x3, then +1 _____ 5. B. divide by 2, then +1 _____ 6. A. squared
_____ 7. B. divide by 4, then -3 _____ 8. A. x5, then -1 _____ 9. E. squared, then +1
_____ 10. C. to the third power _____ 11. A. to the third power, then +2 _____ 12. B. squared
_____ 13. D. divide by 2, +1 _____ 14. C. square fraction (convert to a decimal), then +1
_____ 15. A. equivalent _____ 16. E. divide by 4, then +1 _____ 17. B. to the third power
_____ 18. C. divide by 4, +5 _____ 19. A. x11 _____ 20. B. to the third power

Questions Answered Correctly: _____ out of 20

Number Series, Practice Test 2

_____ 1. D. +39 _____ 2. D. x4

_____ 3. C. every other number is 40; starting from 3, every other number is x2

_____ 4. B. every other number is 22; starting from 78.8, every other number is divided by 2

_____ 5. C. -1, -2, -1, -2, etc. _____ 6. E. +31, +32, +33, +34, +35, etc. _____ 7. B. -1, -1, -2; -1, -1, -2, etc.

_____ 8. E. −1, ×2, −1, ×2, etc. _____ 9. D. ×4, ÷2, ×4, ÷2, etc.

_____ 10. C. numbers in positions 1, 3, 5, etc. (odd) decrease by 2; numbers in positions 2, 4, 6, etc. (even) increase by 2.

_____ 11. A. −3, −3, +1, −3, −3, +1, etc.

_____ 12. B. ×1, ×1, ÷1; ×2, ×2, ÷2; ×3, ×3, ÷3 _____ 13. C. numbers decrease by 3, 4, 5, 6, 7, 8, 9, etc.

_____ 14. A. digits decrease by 1 -and- signs alternate between positive and negative; OR numbers in the odd positions decrease by 2 & numbers in even positions increase by 2

_____ 15. C. starting with 5.5, the number decreases by 2 every other number; starting with -0.5, the number decreases by 1 every other number

_____ 16. B. every other number, starting with -3, is 3x the previous; every other number, starting with -7, increases by 9.

_____ 17. D. ×2, ×3, ×2, ×3, etc. _____ 18. C. -3, +4, -5 | -6, +7, -8 | -9 ,+10, -11

_____ 19. A. -30, +40, -50 | -60, +70, -80 | -90 ,+100, -110 _____ 20. E. -1, +2, -3 | -4, +5, -6 | -7 ,+8, -9

Questions Answered Correctly: _____ out of 20

Check out our other books for COGAT® K to Grade 6

www.GatewayGifted.com

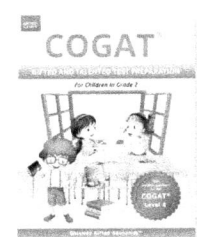